MW01296690

Walking With The Mailman

By Austin Brown

To my wife, without whom this work wouldn't have been possible.

Photographer: Tom Dinkledine

www.dinkledinephotography.com

Many thanks to Tom Dinkledine for willingly subjecting himself to the awful task of trying to persuade an animal to cooperate with a photo shoot. We originally wanted a small Schnauzer by the name of Lucy to pose for the camera and display an angry look. Unfortunately, and much to our chagrin, Lucy proved unimaginably docile, and we suspect torture wouldn't even alter her countenance. So after an hour of much cajoling and pleading, we turned our attention to another dog, an eighty-pound, happy-go-lucky Labrador whose wagging tail threatened to knock over hundreds of dollars of camera equipment. At the end of the day, we just needed him to stand on my hat. But alas, he preferred to sit, and so I want to extend my hearty appreciation to Jacob (the dog's owner) who was willing to hold the rear of his dog while we steadied the front paw. So thank you Tom and Jacob. And thank you, my dear hat, for enduring such humiliation. As for the dogs, I reluctantly say, "Thanks." But don't let it go to your heads. We are not friends.

Cover Design: Bryce Brown

A special thanks to my brother, Bryce, for enduring the minutia of cover design; and especially his ability, through the mystical arts of photo-manipulation, of making that furry brown leg grow longer. You literally saved it. May your Frankensteinian abilities ever increase!

A percentage of the proceeds of this book will be given to the *Be The Match Foundation*®. To learn more about the organization, visit their website at www.BeTheMatchFoundation.org.

Also visit the website: www.walkingwiththemailman.com

The views and opinions expressed here are entirely those of the author and do not necessarily reflect those of the USPS or the *National Marrow Donor Program*.

Some of the names of the people in this work have been changed in order to protect their identity. Since not everything said herein is flattering, I don't want an angry mob showing up outside my house with torches and pitchforks. So any perceived resemblances are, therefore, probably spot on, but should be regarded as merely coincidental.

First Edition

Contents

Many animals were harmed in the making of this book.

Walking With The Mailman

-Introduction-

Ah yes, the mailman. You've seen us out and about before, walking across lawns with our sunglasses in place, bags dangling by our sides, hands full of mail. We're an American icon of sorts, kind of like firemen, though not as cool, and sorta like policemen, though most children aren't itching to grow up and carry mail. Besides the occasional mishap with rifles, people think of the mailman as someone they can trust and look to for directions. Some might also think of Cliff Clavin rambling off a handful of inane facts, or possibly Newman, that chubby guy on Seinfeld who loathes Jerry. A few more fundamentals about the mailman certainly come to mind: they walk in the rain, wear blue uniforms, hand us our bills and, of course, contend with dogs. We're envied in the spring and pitied in the winter, but beyond this, I've found that most people simply aren't aware of the finer points of mail delivery. This is due in part to our sworn secrecy because of the sensitive and highly confidential mail we're required to deliver on a regular basis. No, not really. I just made that up. Actually, I think most people only see the mailman for a brief moment each day and sporadically at that. Therefore they're left to wonder what it must be like to walk from one yard to another continually stepping over doggy landmines for hours on end.

Oh, but not anymore!

Like the contents of a fragile parcel, the mysteries of postal life have at last been shattered, revealing the inner workings in all their brilliant glory. Yes, the letter of truth has finally been delivered to the right place. So for all those who have ever wondered what it must be like for mailmen to brave angry tempests or battle through blizzards, wrestle frothy-mouthed dogs or traverse the lawns of both the marginally normal and the fantastically weird, then this is the book for you. Indeed, you hold in your hands the first ever, officially unofficial publication about mailmen and their daily experiences.

Well, not *all* mailmen, exactly.

Here the reader will follow the story of a young letter carrier trekking along the sidewalks of Indiana, at first quite green- terribly green- but in time growing in maturity, learning the secret arts of blue collar survival amid a land where the average citizen roams wild, unhindered and real. It's my story. It's my true story. And I have chronicled it for the enquiring reader.

Now when I say "story," I should explain something. The structure of this work is more episodic in nature, more like a collection of essays, snapshots of my career. Therefore, I've recorded only those stories that are interesting and humorous. Why? Not only does this make my life seem cooler than it really is, but from a writing standpoint, it was way easier. And that's a good thing. I also like to think that I'm accommodating those with ADD.

So as far as strict chronology is concerned, there is but a general forward progression from the beginning of my career to the present, which is to say that the following events occurred sometime between the early spring of 1995 and today.

But enough talk about the structure. It's high time to begin the postal adventure. So tie up your shoes, grab some sunscreen along with a fresh can of dog mace, and let's go for a walk.

Chapter 1

Deus Ex Machina

[Latin phrase meaning: An improbable solution to an apparently insoluble problem.]

The soft grass felt good under my winter feet as I strolled across the lawn. Spring was waking up from a deep sleep and the whole world seemed to be smiling in response. In this upper class neighborhood the mail weighed heavily on my back, but I really didn't notice it, for it was a gorgeous afternoon, perfect really, and I felt free and light in my short sleeved shirt. I could feel the warmth of the sun on my arms and the forgotten songs of birds filled the air. All was well.

Rarely is a new mailman, a true bottom of the barrel letter carrier with mere crumbs of seniority, assigned such a lush route. But somehow on this particular day the circumstances worked out just right, a sweet providence, perhaps, and City Route One fell to me.

Few routes equal City One. It's a glowing place, a parade of immaculate lawns where one not only catches the fragrant scent of blooming flowers, but the aroma of old money hangs thick in the air.

I'd be prepared to argue that the best relay in our city is located on this route. Maybe the world. It's an enchanting little walk. You follow a quiet, bending road under a high canopy of oaks and maples. As squirrels play in the swaying branches, sunlight dances on the earth below. The houses are all nestled in the woods on one side of the street, which means that when you drop the mail off at the last box, you're free to stroll back in an easy fashion and enjoy the tranquility. This single relay can wash away a week's worth of anxiety.

Later that day, I glanced down at my watch. Ten after three. The work day was nearing its end. Standing at the back of my truck, I examined the last few remaining relays. They were short and sweet.

About an hour to go, I thought to myself, starting to think about my evening plans. I loaded up my bag, grabbed a small parcel, shut the back door and headed off.

This particular relay is "T" shaped. The carrier starts at the bottom of the "T" and follows the shape around to the right, across the top and back down, returning to his truck in about twenty minutes.

All was quiet as I moved from one two-story brick house to the next. I fingered the letters and then the flats, delivered the mail and proceeded on. I fingered the letters, and then the flats, my head lifted up and... I noticed something.

Some distance away, across the street, I distinctly saw a dog running toward me.

Now one must understand that in the animal kingdom there are different running styles to suit different occasions. There is the frightened, full throttle sprint one will see in an animal facing mortal danger. Their faces are full of dread and terror. Sheer panic propels them as they run for their lives.

The dog coming toward me wasn't running like this.

We can also talk about the free spirited gallop. If you picture a giraffe trotting happily about under the African sun with a well pleased look on his face, then you know what I'm talking about. It's the "Hey, let's jog over to this water hole" kind of run.

The dog coming toward me wasn't running like this either.

There is also the "My master is home and I'm running to greet him" kind of run. This one is quite common with dogs. At the sight or sound of their owner, the dog's face is marked with excitement as their tail wildly wags back and forth, "My master is here! My master is here! Go, go! Run!" And with all the animation of an amusement park they slam into their owner, bending back and forth at the midsection like a large bass out of water. A few reassuring pats on their side with a bit of "Good boy, you're a good dog," usually calms the animal slightly.

The dog coming toward me definitely wasn't running like this.

No, his manner of running resembled something altogether different, something far more disturbing, something like the "I'm gonna eat you for lunch" kind of run. It's predatory in nature, ferocious and chilling; like a cheetah bursting out of the tall grass for his prey, his sleek body flexing with each great stride, ears back, eyes focused, his almost gravity-defying speed lifting him off the ground.

Unfortunately, the dog coming toward me was sprinting just like a hungry cheetah.

Fear instantly gripped my heart.

It should be noted that this fear didn't spring so much from the "I'm going to eat you for lunch" kind of run- for I had dealt with that on other occasions- but it sprang from the realization that this wasn't just any old dog coming towards me. It was that creature of postal infamy which mailmen of old have spoken about with great sobriety and earnestness. From the lips of these postal ancients, terrifying traditions have been passed down so as to warn and prepare green little carriers for just such an occasion as this. Now my time had come, and I could only stand there with wide, shock-filled eyes at what was rushing towards me. For there, now only 70 feet away, was the awful and dreaded pit bull.

Oh Mommy, the pit bull; the *Rippus Leggus Offitus*, the most feared of all dogs. It's said that this fiend has been forged out of the very pits of hell. I mean really, can we call something that's half devil a breed of dog? We've heard the stories about their "lockjaw" and how someone will have to use a crowbar to free the poor victim from the dog's mouth. We've heard the stories of cops shooting the animal five times in the face to no avail. We've heard how they've been bred to continue fighting through dehydration, broken limbs and even decapitation. And now, here in what should have been one of the most unlikely neighborhoods, I was standing directly in the crosshairs of a very, very ticked off pit bull.

It's funny how quickly one can forget the pleasures of the day.

So there I stood frozen in the middle of a well manicured lawn watching this dog barrel towards me. A deep chill ran up my spine, and I could feel the blood draining from my body as my mind raced for answers.

"Oh, no..." I murmured.

In a flash, my mind began to operate more rationally. One word came to me, *Mace!* My hand dropped to grab the good old trusty can of dog spray at my side, but to my absolute horror, it was gone.

Gone! How was it gone!?! I always carry mace. Where is it!?! Did it fall off?

Oh, no!

It's hard to describe the flood of emotions that hit me all at once, though it felt as if I had been suddenly struck by the blast of a shotgun with every little pellet cutting through me producing a different effect: shock, terror, sorrow, anger... But most clearly felt of all was something like the sensation of being buck naked. It was an acute awareness of just how poorly equipped we humans are for combat, in comparison to animals, anyway. My finger nails tend to be too long, but they would hardly pass as claws. I suppose I do have a strong bite, but it's terribly unwieldy. I can't outrun the dog, I don't have wings, and I can't even crawl up inside a shell. I'm just a thin, white, juicy steak with a head.

As the dog closed in, I had to make a decision. Would I run or make a stand? The thought jumped into my head: *Just kick that thing as hard as you can!*

That's it! I'll kick it!

Kick it? What was I thinking? What a moron! Was I really going to put my leg out there so that Lockjaw could clamp onto it forever? I might as well set my leg on a plate with a fork and knife and hand it to him.

It was too late for further deliberation. I had made my choice.

As the dog came in hard, I pulled back my leg and shot it out with all the might I could muster. I suppose someone who knows a thing or two about Karate would say that I attempted, at least in theory, a front snap kick. As this "front snap kick" went out, I actually felt it connect. To my utter amazement, it was a solid hit and the dog, well, at this point I wish I could boast of having kicked the dog so hard that I sent him flying through the air in a back flip, but it was much more modest than that. I had merely deflected him. The kick simply kept him from slamming into me. But it worked. So there he stood, about four feet away, momentum gone, snarling something vicious.

If I thought the dog looked ticked off before, I could now see hell-fire blazing in his eyes. And with those eyes, he communicated to me one very clear message, "Bad idea, mailman. Now you gonna die."

I wish I could say that I followed up my "front snap kick" with a roundhouse or something Jackie Chan-ish, but the whole thought of making a stand seemed like a really bad idea. I still had my right leg and I liked it that way. So the decision to run came quite easily. In a flash, I turned and began to run away like a little girl.

There then followed something most unfortunate.

Talk about being at the wrong place at the wrong time, but I didn't realize that there was a street sign only a few feet behind me, and so when I spun around, of course with my head turned to watch the dog, I proceeded to slam right into the metal pole with a "thud." Yep, my face and shoulder smacked right into that stupid thing, which pretty much ended my mad dash in an instant. It had the effect of spinning me about so that I was facing Lockjaw again. His eyes gave me a slightly new message, "Real slick, stupid. Now you gonna die."

At the Post Office, sometimes we're required to watch instructional videos about safety. Early in the morning, the supervisor will yell out, "Gather round everybody- Safety talk!" With a few protesting groans we grab our stools and lazily plop down in front of a 24-inch Zenith. As the supervisor fumbles around with the remote, we rub the morning sleep from our eyes and try to get comfortable. The blue screen of death flickers a bit and the movie starts up.

On one such morning the video began with the frozen image of a snarling and wild eyed German Shepherd staring us down. Intense music blared out of the speakers and a bold red title slowly took form. It read, "When Dogs Attack."

That's funny. They didn't say, "If Dogs Attack." They said, "When Dogs Attack." Is this the Post Office's not so subtle way of telling us, "That's right boys and girls, sooner or later they're gonna jump ya, and we can't afford for you to sit in a hospital, so pay attention."

It's interesting that they also didn't say, "If A *Dog* Attacks," but they said, "When *Dogs* Attack." Good grief, can we expect to be assaulted by a whole pack of dogs?

Needless to say, the video definitely had our attention.

There then followed the all too typical cheesy acting which seems to be a universal given for such productions. Some of the guys chuckled and elbowed each other as we watched a smiling mailman walk down the street and get ambushed by a lunging German Shepherd. Just before the guy was devoured, the picture froze and some instructional bullets highlighted the proper procedure for dealing with aggressive dogs.

The first one said, "Don't panic."

Don't panic? You've got a hell hound trying to tear you apart and you're not supposed to panic? The room was beginning to liven up with laughter.

The next bullet read, "Use your spray as a defense."

Great idea! But what the heck are you supposed to do when your dog spray magically disappears?

Another bullet came into view, "Use your bag as a shield."

The video proceeded to demonstrate the technique. The mailman, who by now had an incredibly overacted expression of fear on his face, stuck his bag out in front of him and held the dog at bay. It worked wonderfully! The dog was thwarted and the mailman escaped from the German Shepherd's clutches. Simple as that.

That was it! All I had to do was use my bag as a shield and all would be just fine. And so that's exactly what I did next.

The dog's muscles tightened as he prepared to charge in for the kill, but just as he was about to pounce, I pushed out my blue mailbag like a gladiator using his shield to deflect an incoming sword. I couldn't believe it, but it worked. It deterred the dog. The pit bull could have easily swallowed my bag whole if he so chose, but for some reason he was a little confused by the action and chose instead to try to circle around and flank me. But with every dart to the left and jump to the right, I pivoted and wheeled around to meet him. I held out my bag like a crucifix and marveled at how the vampric beast kept his distance.

This was all good and dandy, but what next? All my attention had to remain focused on keeping that dog in front of me. I didn't look around for a tree to climb. I didn't think to yell for help. I didn't try to steal a look at the ground for a missing can of dog spray. I could only play defense. But I knew that I couldn't keep it up much longer.

What happened next still astonishes me to this day. Out of the corner of my eye, I caught sight of something moving in our direction. Daring a look, I saw a large, grey-colored Buick heading straight for us. Inside I could see a little old man with a plain hat, both hands on the steering wheel at ten and two, picking up speed as he was obviously going to try to run us over. Wait! No, not *us*, but *the dog*! He must have seen what was going on as he was cruising down the top of the "T" and decided to change his coordinates for the pit bull. He was trying to save me. He was my *Deus Ex Machina*! And so, while laying on the horn, he drove right up into the grass in order to spear the dog.

I jumped to the side and the pit bull backpedaled with a confused expression on his face. As the Buick's horn thundered, the dog displayed complete alarm. The old boat revved and lurched forward with threatening jerks as the driver slammed the brakes, pushed the pedal, slammed the brakes and revved the engine. The dog had no idea what to do. Who would? I hardly knew what to do. It isn't every day that you see an old man drive across someone's yard in order to squash a dog.

I stood there dumbfounded for a moment and then realized that gawking wasn't the smartest thing to do. I had a clear opening of escape, and so I took it.

In my line of work it's always good to remember that someone at any given time may be watching you- a chance glance out an upstairs window, a peering look down a side street. I wonder if on this day anyone had the privilege of watching my struggle come to an end. Perhaps only the birds and the squirrels saw the man in the blue uniform running frantically down the street toward the parked truck. They would have watched his run stutter with short hops as his hand worked hard at pulling out some keys. They finally would have witnessed his dive into the truck and the slam of the door. Peering down from their branch, they would have seen a very pale mailman panting heavily with a look of disbelief on his face. And if they looked very carefully, they may have noticed that he still clutched in his left hand a bundle of letters that were still somehow neatly in order.

Chapter 2

The Miracle of a Postmaster's Ailing Back

"Gravitation cannot be held responsible for people falling in love."

-Albert Einstein-

The female instructor, with her clear, monotone voice continued, "And when we tell you 'time,' you are to put your pencils down and await further instructions. I repeat: there is to be nothing done after time has been called."

The day of the postal exam had finally arrived, and as I sat amongst the three hundred or so other people looking to land a job with the US Postal Service, I could feel the anxiety building within me. It's surely an overstatement to say that everything in the universe was riding on my performance during that two-hour period, but it felt like it. I was nineteen years old and barely qualified to flip cheeseburgers. I had ended my high school career with an impressive 2.1 GPA (thank goodness for all those art classes), and, here's the big one, I was madly in love and engaged to the daughter of Pastor H.F. Drye, a practical man of German descent who greatly valued hard work and commitment. Over the years he had dealt with a lot of couples experiencing marital problems and knew how important financial stability is to a fledgling marriage. Needless to say, he would never be as charmed by my sappy love poems as his daughter. Therefore, if I was going to have any hope of freeing my future father-in-law from an addiction to Rolaids, and if I was going to be able to provide something other than a cardboard box as a home for my fiancé, then I needed to find a good job and pronto. The problem, of course, is that good jobs exist for people who have good skills, and for some reason, my exceptional talent at beating video games wasn't something I could put on my resume. Therefore, I had to fall back on my fast food experience, which, for some other reason, didn't seem to impress too many employers either.

I could say that I had some factory experience. The place I worked at was called Carpal Tunnel Manufacturing. While sitting at a long table next to women with colossally large rear ends, my job was to pick up a green wire thingamajiggy from out of a hamper full of thousands of other green wire thingamajiggies, measure it to make sure it wasn't too long or too short, and then throw it into either a box labeled "good" or a box labeled "bad." The boredom I experienced there was so intense that I genuinely wondered if it might lead to internal hemorrhaging. So the strategy was to gorge oneself with as much water as is humanly possible, so that after about twenty minutes I would have to go to the bathroom. My breaking point came while seated next to a woman muttering inane sounds. She was sweating profusely and clearly agitated. At one point, she turned to face me, eyes wild, face feverish, and said, "I just want to kill that woman... Who does she think she is?" She then returned to measuring the green wires. I waited a while and then made a mad dash for the door; never, ever returning to that horrible place. Since that happened on the third day of my employment there, I figured that I should probably just leave that bit of job experience off my resume... which meant that my personal marketability was outstandingly unimpressive, and which also meant that things were looking really bleak for Romeo.

But my prospects soon changed when a Postmaster's ailing back provided me a glimmer of hope.

One day, the local postmaster decided to pay a visit to my father, one of several chiropractors in the area. My father, naturally quite concerned about my future prospects, inquired about potential employment with the US Postal Service. While the postmaster was lying prone, face down on the table, vulnerable and unable to flee, my dad asked, "So what would my son have to do in order to (Crunch! Snap!) get his foot in the door with the Postal Service?"

"Well, he's going to have to take an exam. But listen, today's the last day to sign up- (Pop!) Oh! That was the spot, Doc- listen, if he misses this round, it could be a couple years before another exam cycle opens up. He's got to get over to Rossville by five o' clock and sign up today. "

"Five o' clock?" My father said with a jolt, looking at his watch.

"Yep, five o' clock today. My wife's the Postmaster over there, so have your son tell her I sent him."

Later that afternoon, when I returned home from slaving away at Wendy's, my dad told me that I needed to bust it over to Rossville and sign up for a postal exam. That sounded cool, but if you know anything about working at a fast food joint, then you know that a person smells absolutely horrific after a long day's work around bubbling grease pits. But if I was going to make it in time, I had to leave right away. So I left immediately, Wendy's uniform still pasted on, windows rolled fully down, in search of the Post Office in the little town of Rossville, thinking along the way what it must be like to be a mailman.

Three months later, I was taking the test.

The female instructor continued, "You are going to have three minutes to study all the addresses and names written in a box. After that you are going to be asked a series of questions about the items in that box. Try to recall what you have seen and answer my questions accurately." There was a pause and then silence pervaded the room. I could feel my heart thumping with anticipation. Looking up from her stop watch, she announced, "You may begin."

The sound of several hundred papers could be heard flipping over. I eagerly turned mine over and immediately saw a large box located in the upper half of the page. Located within that box were an assortment of numbers, names and addresses, all of which were jumbled about in no apparent order. I saw a George Marshall in the upper left hand corner, a zip code in the middle and a partial address, 212 E Melbourne Ave, near the bottom. There were more than I had anticipated, so I steadied myself and tried to focus.

Focus, Austin, focus! I thought to myself, trying to push my mind to greater depths of concentration. Have you ever been in a situation where you're trying to perform a difficult task, maybe a piano recital, or giving a speech, perhaps, and you realize that you're actually more aware of your thinking about your thinking than the actual task at hand? That's what happened to me. As my eyes scanned over the various items, my inner self kept analyzing how my thoughts were doing and updated me accordingly. *Ok, look at the right hand row and concentrate. Think Austin... No, quit thinking about how you're looking at them and remember them. Austin, quit talking to yourself and think! No, you're still doing it... Ah, I'm doomed! Focus!!!"* At that moment it seemed as if all those teachers who once told me, "Austin, if you would just apply yourself! You're better than this; apply yourself young man," were forming an "L" on their foreheads, conceding at last that I should have ridden the short bus.

"Time's up."

Audible groans echoed throughout the room. Everyone reluctantly turned over their papers and shuffled them off to the end of their table where they were then gathered up and taken away. With a fresh sheet of paper situated before us, we began to be questioned.

"Question one: Was Belfort an avenue or street?"

Somehow I remembered that. It was definitely a street.

"Question two: Were there one or two zip codes in the far left column?"

Sweet mother of Pearl, I remembered that one too.

On went the questions, some of which I decidedly did not know, but the majority of which I was pretty sure I had right.

That's part of the beauty of the Postal exam. You can have little to no marketable skills whatsoever, be an otherwise complete dolt, but if your mind is naturally disposed towards remembering random names and numbers, then your future with those who have the eagle emblem is bright. For me, things were looking up.

Another part of the test had two parallel columns of addresses running down the center of the page. All you had to do was answer whether or not the two addresses on each line were the same or different. One might be 2510 E. Thorton Street, while the other is 2510 W. Thorton Street. Those two are clearly different. The catch is that you only have a short amount of time to complete the entire list of comparisons. And the list is very long.

When the instructor told us to put our pencils down, there were mixed reactions at my table. Some wore painful looks, while others leaned back in their chairs with confident, almost cheery expressions smeared across their faces. It was patently obvious who finished this segment before time ran out and who didn't. I didn't quite make it, but I did feel confident that what I had completed was error-free because of a conscious choice to go with quality over quantity.

The last part, the strangest in my opinion, tested how well one can listen and follow directions.

"I will tell you to perform a certain task once and only once," began the instructor. "There will be no repeating the commands and there will be no pausing. When I have finished all of my instructions, you will be told what to do with your tests." Once again the woman paused and everyone in the room sat motionless, as still as stones, their gazes firmly fixed on the woman.

She suddenly began, "Pick up your pencil and draw a small circle in the middle of the blank piece of paper in front of you. Now write a lower case "n" inside of that circle. You are now required to draw a line underneath the circle. In the upper right hand corner, not the lower left hand corner, nor the bottom right hand corner, I want you to..." On and on went the directions. By the end, my paper looked like the walls of some Egyptian tomb, a variety of strange symbols and markings covering nearly every square inch of the white surface. When we were told to write our names at the top of the paper, right in the middle, that concluded the test, and we were politely asked to leave.

The most difficult part was over, or at least so I thought. Next came the waiting period. You're dying to know how well you did and whether or not you'll be seated toward the top of the hiring chain. The Post Office first considers the highest scores and then descends down the line; maybe reaching the mediocre scores, maybe not. It all depends on the number of job openings.

During the painful waiting process, my mother, while running errands, decided to pull over and ask a mailman how likely it would be for her son to get a job carrying the mail.

He asked, "Is he a veteran?"

"No."

"Then his chances are slim to none."

That's not what we were hoping to hear, but there's a lot of truth to the statement. Veterans automatically score 5 to 10 more points on the test depending upon how many years they've served their country. So basically, if they score a ninety on their test, their service could propel them on up to a perfect score of a hundred. I think it's a magnanimous policy and wouldn't change a thing if given the opportunity, but it did mean that I needed to score well if I was going to be noticed.

Finally, after much waiting, I received my test results in the mail. Tearing it open, I eagerly looked it over. I scored a ninety-one. Word on the street led me to believe that it was a good score, but I didn't know if it was good enough. Ultimately, receiving a call was the only sure sign.

So as time continued to roll by without receiving any further word, the real test of patience began. I was starving for answers. Will they call? How many people scored better than me? Might I have to wait a month before hearing anything? Two months? Six months? Questions like these felt like hungry rats running around inside my head gnawing away my thoughts, burrowing tunnels right through my peace of mind. Everyday a sense of expectancy swirled within me, an anticipation of good news loomed before me, but no word, nothing.

But then it happened. The magical phone call finally came.

"We would like you to come on in for an interview. Would Thursday at 3 o' clock be good?"

"Perfect."

Things weren't perfect, however. The Postmaster told me that there was someone else, an older man, a veteran, who scored slightly higher than I did on the test and that he would have first dibs on the job. But there was a catch. They didn't want to hire him. His knees were giving him trouble and they knew it. That's a *huge* red flag. Solid knees are as good as gold at the Post Office, and those with poor ones are sent off to the tar pits. So when they looked at my fresh legs they said to themselves, "Well, Getty up! There's at least twenty years of surgery free work in those skinny things. Let's put a saddle on that boy." They ended up sending faulty-knee-man off to a clinic where they ran the poor guy through a series of strenuous stress tests, probably making him run the equivalent of the Hawaii Ironman on a treadmill. At about the same time, they sent me off to see Dr. Faheem Rahkshaw for my physical. He simply said, "Would you please bend your knee? Very good. Open up and say, 'Ahh.' Very good then. Cough twice, ok, you very healthy. Now you go, Mr. Brown."

With that stamp of approval, as well as a report that faulty-knee man failed his test, I was hired.

The euphoric jubilation that erupted from my family can still be heard echoing across the waters of Lake Michigan to this very day. Most notably, and most understandably, the happiest lark of them all would have to be my father-in-law. For a solid two years, he told anyone with half an interest, and with a face that shone with the brightness of heaven, that his son-in-law was a genuine mailman, often adding, "It's a good job- secure, very secure. A lot of people would love to have a job like that. Just love to have it."

He clearly said this as much for my sake as anything. He feared that I wouldn't comprehend how blessed I was to have this job and quit for some dumb reason. The only practical thing I could do to comfort his uneasy spirit was express, with all the terrific enthusiasm I could muster, just how thankful I was. It wasn't hard though, because I was truly thankful. God, in His good providence, orchestrated a way for me to marry my high school sweetheart, and that's what I wanted most.

So it was an amazing time for me. All within the span of a couple months, I began a career as a mailman, purchased a home and married my lovely Rebekah. Life was sweet.

But then I actually began delivering the mail.

Chapter 3

Working Hard for a Check

"Welfare is hated by those who administer it, mistrusted by those who pay for it and held in contempt by those who receive it."

-Peter C Goldmark, Jr.

"Hey, Helen," I asked with my finger on the modified schedule, "I thought I was supposed to be on City 20?" The supervisor looked up from the computer screen, flashed a look like, "Huh?" cleared away the expression with a shake, then said, "There was a sick call. You're on City 11 now."

She promptly returned to the computer and I looked over at the vacant case of City 11. I was still new at the Post Office and so moving around to different routes meant unfamiliarity. Unfamiliarity is a bad thing.

Every morning we carriers have to "case up" our mail. This means that we have to take a pile of unsorted letters and flats (catalogs, magazines, etc.) and match them to an address slot in our case. This puts them in order. Once they're in order, we're then able to pull the mail down and bundle them into relays that are sequenced for walking. So imagine yourself picking up a letter that reads, "222 E Main." Now find the one slot for that letter and do this a few hundred more times. As you can imagine, if you're unfamiliar with the route, this means that you can look forward to spinning around with a dumb expression on your face, as you scan each row for the letter's correct spot- some 550 different slots spread out across a three-sided box of sorts.

With a sigh, I walked over to the case and gave the dangling string to the overhead lights a tug.

Right after I slid in my first magazine, another letter carrier, a man of exquisitely short stature, poked his head around and said with a wry smile, "City 11 on the first of the month, huh?" He chuckled then immediately added, "Have fun." He disappeared from view but I could still hear his suspiciously sardonic laugh as he clicked on some lights.

At the time, I wasn't sure what to make of the semi-cryptic statement, nor his enigmatic chuckle. Since I was young and healthy, a part of the working class and still quite unaware of all the ins and outs of mail delivery, I had no idea what it meant to be delivering the mail on the first of the month, and I equally had no idea what it meant to be on City 11 on the first of the month. What it meant was that I was going be delivering the coveted SSI check to some very, very eager recipients.

The SSI check traces its origin back to President Nixon. He started a government program designed to help the aged, blind, disabled or poor (it should be noted that this is distinct from Social Security). Basically, if you're hurt or poor or old you can apply for some benefits, and if you can convince them that you are a worthy beneficiary, then you'll begin to receive a modest amount of money each month to help you get by. The numbers fluctuate each year, and it varies state by state, but in December of 2004, there were some 96,000 individuals in Indiana who received the federally administered SSI payments. 90,000 of these fell into the category of the disabled or blind. Of these 90,000, some 65,000 are under the age of 65. I'm pretty sure that a good percentage of this last figure live somewhere on City Route 11.

Delivering the mail on the first of the month is kind of like the movie "Night of the Living Dead." Strange people come from out of the shadows and lumber down the street to find their SSI checks. They grope around the neighborhood in search of your truck, sometimes in packs, and when they find it they hang out there until you come strolling back. As you finish off the relay you will see some crusty guy pacing around the back of your truck, or a beat-up Chevette will be parked in front with the head of a woman hanging out, her best smile pasted on. Some variation of the following question inevitably follows, "Can I get my check, please?"

Sometimes they leave off the "please," sometimes they preface the question with niceties like, "Well, good morning, mailman, how are you doing?" or "Boy, am I glad to have run into you..." Many times they will tack on an explanatory note with an air of urgency, "I've got to run out of town, there's been a family emergency..." or "Jonathan's birthday is today, and I really need to get my check so I can buy him this one really cool toy that....'

The sad reality is that many of these people run off to buy lottery tickets or pick up some smokes. On more than one occasion, after having been told that they were heading out of town and thus needed their check early, I'd later catch them coming out of a gas station with a handful of scratch-offs. As one smacks a fresh pack of cigarettes against their palm, the other can be seen scratching away at a string of Lucky Sevens with their last quarter. It's really annoying to think that you're helping fund this kind of behavior by simply showing up to work. I mean really, I'm out here breaking my back so they can smoke a pack of Camels and watch Days of our Lives? After about the second time you get pestered by some of these folks, you're real tempted to interrupt their story and ask with a concerned look, "You look like you're in a hurry- running late for work?"

One could say that I'm well acquainted with the strategies and practices of SSI recipients now, but back when I was casing up City 11 on that early summer morning of long ago, I had no idea what was coming down the pike. I certainly knew that the route was situated in a rough neighborhood, an old train stop area formerly known as a red light district, but it didn't occur to me that maybe, just maybe there's a connection between low income areas and SSI checks. Needless to say, I hardly expected to be the most popular person in the neighborhood that day.

As I turned off the engine and slid open the door, having arrived at my first park point, an older man wearing a flannel shirt meandered over to greet me. He broke off from what appeared to be a casual conversation with another couple standing nearby.

"Well, hey there." He said as he drew near.

"Hi."

The older man rubbed his chin, "Where's Jerry?"

Jerry was the regular on this route; a short, quirky guy that loved to tell jokes, belt out hilarious limericks and invigorate parties with his wit and humor. In the years to come, he would refer to me as "The boil on the butt of all mailmen everywhere." If you're going to have a moniker that sticks around, this may not be your first choice, but coming from Jerry, it was actually a term of endearment. He even named a small doll at home "Austin." It was his golden retriever's toy. He would look at his dog, Riley, and ask, "Where's Austin? Go get 'em boy. Get 'em." Riley would then spring off in search of the Austin doll, snatch him up in his mouth and violently shake it around for fun. Jerry thought this was great.

Jerry was the regular and was also the one who had called in sick, so I answered the man briefly, saying, "He's off today."

The older man nodded. I could see a thought forming in his mind. After a short pause, the man dipped his hands into his blue jeans, leaned forward slightly and asked, "You don't suppose I could get you to give me my mail early, do you?" The couple standing behind the guy watched with interest.

It occurred to me that if I agreed to meet his request, I was going to have to dig around in the back of my truck. This would mean climbing over parcels, moving around heavy trays and sifting through a labyrinth of letters and magazines in order to find this guy's mail. Had I taken more time to consider this fact I might have declined, but under the pressure I simply stammered, "Um, do you have I.D.?"

The man smiled and worked his wallet free. The other couple knew they had a green light and moved in. And so I dug around in the back of my truck in search of their mail. I couldn't help but notice that each had received a small, blue letter from the government- a letter which, quite evidently, brought them incredible delight. They were transfixed by it, overjoyed and relieved at all at once. There was something about the way they held it and gazed upon it that made me think of how Gollum would tenderly caress his ring and whisper in a slightly maniacal tone, "My Precious... My Precious..."

"Thanks, mailman." And with that, they left.

Ten minutes hadn't even passed before another person pulled up in a beater that had lost its new car smell a couple millennia ago.

The man hung his arm out the window and asked, "Hey bro, I'm, uh, heading out of town and wondered if I could get my mail." If anything was apparent, it was that this car would be lucky to make it to the end of the street, let alone down a highway. But I wasn't going to make a fuss, so I asked the man if he had some I.D. He responded cheerfully, "Yeah, right here."

Once again I crawled around in the back of my truck looking for some guy's mail, and once again, I noticed the same little, blue letter. When I handed it to him, he blurted out, "Ah, there is it. Hey, see ya around, mailman." As he drove off, it was beginning to become clear that there was something special about those blue letters. I didn't know what it was exactly, but I was tired of being hassled and so I made up my mind to turn down the next person who might bug me for their mail. Looking back, it's pretty funny that I had made this decision before Mrs. Mosley came around.

"Well, hey there, baby," said Mrs. Mosley, as she pulled up beside me.

The first thing that I noticed wasn't the silver, four-door idling next to me, nor the little old lady in the passenger seat, nor the two odd looking fellows in the back, but I was immediately struck by one very prominent, glittering, gold tooth in the center of the driver's wide, toothy smile. The owner of that tooth was Mrs. Mosley, a plump, but not too plump, middle-aged black woman with large engaging eyes. Just north of her shimmering smile flourished a mass of dark hair, which was partially contained under a tightly wrapped red handkerchief, with not a few wild strands spilling down her back, curling freely. In the passenger seat sat a tiny woman well into her seventies. Her face was filled to the brim with wrinkles and curly white hair sprang out from her small head in all directions. She stared at me with twitching, pursed lips. In the back were two, thin, white guys that immediately struck me as strange. One of them had a long face and kept staring down at his feet, while the other looked about with a mouth that seemed to hang a little too wide open for normal intelligence. One might suppose his name to be Jethro, or Jim-Bob, or something.

"Where's my Jerry at?" asked Mrs. Mosley with searching eyes, as though he were to be found somewhere off in the distance, perhaps hiding behind a bush.

I explained that he had called in sick. She nodded her head as she digested the information.

"You don't suppose we might get some checks, do ya? Jerry always has'em for us."

I hesitated as I tried to think how I was going to tell her no. There's something about four people, well, three people, for the one guy was still staring at the floor, anyway, there's something compelling about three people looking at you with eager expressions as they wait for you to say, "Well, sure, Jerry laid down a contingency plan for just such an occasion as this. Here you go- three checks. Have a nice day." It was also difficult for this nineteen-year-old to say no to a grown woman who simply wanted her mail early. And there was something almost hypnotic about the gold tooth which had surfaced again on a fresh smile. I felt as if I couldn't resist agreeing to her request. But even with all those forces pressing down on me, I managed to squeak out, "I'm- I'm sorry, but, uh... well, I can't."

"WAH-chew talkin-bout, mailman?" She exclaimed.

That's all it took, really, just one well placed, high pitched question and I was ready to give up. I mean seriously, what *was* I talking about? It was certainly within my jurisdiction to decline her request, for it does waste time to go spelunkering around for someone's mail (and time is money), but it wasn't like I *couldn't* do it. I could. And besides, I had already done it several times that day. Nevertheless, I found a measure of fortitude remaining in my spongy spine and stood firm one more time.

"Look, I'm sorry, but you're just going to have to wait until I get to your house."

She stared hard at me.

I shrugged my shoulders as if to say, "I'm sorry."

Mrs. Mosley turned and looked out the windshield. As she stared out the window, she made a strange sucking sound with her mouth as if she were trying to dislodge something out from between her teeth. She started to say something but her voice was suddenly drowned out by the roar of her car as she slammed the gas pedal down and screeched off. I may have caught a glimpse of a middle finger amid all the commotion, but it's more likely that Darrel and Darrel were trying to get a hold of something as they sped off. I'm just not sure.

There's a great deal more to say about Mrs. Mosley, and in time we'll return to her, but for now it's sufficient to point out that this kind of behavior is completely normal and should be expected when checks are withheld. Just be aware that some will prove more confrontational, some will plead their cases at greater lengths, some will whine and some will turn wonderfully creative or possibly guilt trip you into giving them their mail early. On one occasion, a woman brought a fussy baby along with her, saying that she needed her check so she could buy diapers. I seriously doubted the claim, but who's going to turn down a mother requesting that? Hey, if she was playing me and was willing to go to those extremes, then fine, she wins. More power to her. But she had better not let me catch her with a quick pick.

Now before closing out this chapter, I suppose there might be some who will find my generalizations here disappointing, perhaps a little too harsh or unsympathetic to the needs of hurting people. Well, I certainly don't want to give the impression that I think *all* SSI recipients are moochers or irresponsible. No, no. I am far more balanced in my perspective than that. So let me just set the record straight. In all my years, I can definitely think of two or three worthy cases. No wait! Maybe four! Yeah, I can think of four. Definitely four.

Chapter 4

The Enemy

The faults of the dog are many. He is vainer than man,
singularly greedy of notice, singularly intolerant of ridicule,
suspicious like the deaf, jealous to the degree of frenzy, and radically
devoid of truth. The day of an intelligent small dog is passed in the
manufacture and the laborious communication of falsehood; he lies
with his tail, he lies with his eye, he lies with his protesting paw; and
when he rattles his dish or scratches at the door his purpose is other
than appears.

-Robert Louis Stevenson-

It's true. Dogs are nuts. And when I say that they are nuts, I don't mean that they are kind of wacky, but that they are actually clinically crazy. Now I'm aware that if you read through some of the more scholarly literature out there on dogs, such as Bruce Fogle's work, *Understanding the Dog's Mind*, or Stanley Coren's, *How Dog's Think*, or even the book by Vilmos Csanyi, *If Dog's Could Talk*, they won't come right out and tell you that dogs are nuts. But I do. And that's part of what makes this cutting edge science.

I deal with these ankle biters seven hours a day, five days a week, year after year. This means that I'm able to provide the general public with a fresh perspective, one that is completely objective and free from the taint of bias. So as an expert on this subject, there are two things I want you to know:

1.   Dogs are depraved.
2.   Dogs hate the mailman with all their being.

I know that most people have some general idea about the dog's dislike for the mailman, but it should be stressed that just as

27

Beowulf had his Grendel, Captain Ahab his pearly white Moby Dick and the young Hebrew, David, his Philistine giant, so too the mailman has his dark and carnivorous enemy, the dog.

No doubt some of you will have a hard time accepting this fact, or will at least feel as if I'm exaggerating the point. "Yes, yes, I'm sure the mailman has a run in with a dog now and then," someone will say, "But what is all this talk of epic foe and dark adversary?" I readily confess that the relationship between the mailman and the dog might appear only mildly contentious, but I must stress with all sobriety that things aren't as you might think. Just as the untrained eye misses a poker tell, so too the common American often overlooks significant details which chart out a more deep seated strife which exists between the mailman and the dog.

I am also well aware that there is a proverbial and generally accepted axiom that the dog is man's best friend. But I can assure you that the gentleman who first quipped these words was no letter carrier. It's impossible! Unthinkable, I tell you! For had he been of such stock the entire phrase would have been inverted to aptly express a more profound contempt and scorn which only the cat could possibly appreciate and enjoin. Now I don't think of myself as one of those conspiracy theory types, but it is more than likely that this idea was first introduced and promulgated by the dog itself, or at least by those who stand in collusion with such animals. For I'm prepared to argue that just as the Devil arrays himself as an angel of light, so too the dog conceals his true personality and devilish motives from those closest to him.

That's why you need me to help you see the truth. So lend me your patient ear. Hear my case, and if at the end you aren't convinced, consider me crazy.

But first allow me to anticipate a question. There might be those of careful judgment who may want to know if I think there are any good dogs at all. They will want to ask, "Are there no exceptions, Mr. Mailman? Is there not one good dog in the whole wide world?" A certain statistical probability compels me to admit to there being at least one good dog, but note that this is like asking if there is at least one tender-hearted terrorist. Or would we dare ask if there is at least one Boogieman with a nightlight? The question is clearly absurd, so I will only provide this one response.

There may be a relatively cool spot on the sun, but even then the heat contained in that one small flare is capable of engulfing an entire continent. This is to say that there may be a relatively good dog out there, but shades of depravity are of little practical consequence, really.

Those of you who are acquainted with history or ancient literature will already know how low the opinions of dogs are. It is an incontrovertible fact that dogs have been considered brutish and have been associated with things vile or immoral. In the Holy Scriptures themselves, one will find mention of the lion, the lamb, the cow, the bear, the wolf, and other such animals, as inhabiting the New Heavens and the New Earth. But there is no mention of the dog there, only silence. Instead the Scriptures associate the dog with the impurity and utter sinfulness of those given over to the outer darkness of hell itself. In common parlance the term dog is used as a kind of curse word. One pronounces another the son of a dog in heat. Or if someone really wants to insult a girl's appearance, they refer to her as a dog. Servility, wicked behavior, immorality, ugliness, these are the connotations attending the word "dog."

But not all people are familiar with ancient literature, and so I need to present a more pedestrian argument. Let's consider the dog's behavior. Now I don't want to indulge in vulgarity here, but a certain measure of plain talk is required to make my point. Consider how a dog will feast upon his, let us say, posterior regions. The dog happily licks these parts, even in public, and betrays absolutely no signs whatsoever that he finds the smells and tastes located there less than savory. In fact, he seems to enjoy them immensely. Polite people sit in public and read the paper or sip on coffee, but the dog uses his tongue as a device to explore those recesses of his body that should remain in secret. And after a good buttock sandwich or possibly some road kill desert, the dog then proceeds to shower its owner with kisses, lapping his scratchy tongue all over her face. And if this isn't enough, many dogs take no notice of trampling around in their own doo doo, whereupon they enter their master's home and immediately snuggle up with them on the couch, or even in the very bed in which they sleep.

Shall I discuss the dog's manner of greeting? Instead of shaking hands with their fellow canines, they choose to sniff each other's rear ends. What is that all about? And dare I mention the sexual habits of the dog? Would you have me describe the indecencies with which the dog will openly engage? Shall I write about the strange, smelly rituals dogs perform as a kind of doggy foreplay? Oh, I dare not. Suffice it to say that the dog is a perverted creature, second only to the monkey... maybe.

And shall we not judge a tree by its fruit? Do not actions speak louder than words? I tell you the truth; these indecent practices provide us with a direct window into the hearts of these animals. And when we peer into that porthole, we will at once see a vast array of ungodly desires that, when beheld, extinguish all our doubts concerning the purity and goodness of the dog.

Dear friends, carefully consider my words. Digest them. Take heed, for it could very well be the case that lying next to you right now is not a sweet, reliable friend, but rather a cunning beast capable of great deception. You may very well be a little insect caught in his web.

So consider yourself warned, and trust the insights of a mailman, for he has seen the true face of your pet, and it isn't pretty. It isn't pretty at all.

If there's one thing that a dog can do well, it's yapping. From the very moment we mailmen shut our first mailbox until the last piece of mail has been delivered, our poor ears are bombarded with every imaginable woof, ruff, bow-wow, yip, yap and howl for hours on end. Those who own dogs know this is true. But it probably hasn't occurred to them that their house is merely one noisy stop along a long chain of equally noisy stops. Allow me to paint a picture.

After hopping out of the Postal truck and loading up my bag, I begin walking down the sidewalk, sucking in the morning air through my nose, gearing up for a new day's walk. Almost immediately the sound of yapping can be heard to my right. A small dog behind a white picket fence can be seen running back and forth, panting and barking, hopping in the air. When I look across the street, I can see Mrs. Benish's brown terrier through her bay window. He's standing atop her floral couch, legs rigid, head jerking forward with each muffled bark. Far off in the distance, the long drawn out, "Ahrrrrr, ahrrrrr," of the Beagle begins to sound as he blindly responds to the excitement of his furry friends. The growing commotion inspires yet another dog in the distance to start up, "Arf, arf, arf – Arf, arf, arf." Later on, while standing near Mr. Thompson's front door, something like the sound of a tremendous struggle, almost as if two rhino's were wrestling, can be heard on the other side of the door. A large dog is going berserk, throwing the full weight of its body around like a maniac in a padded room, rattling the hinges and knocking dust off the door frame. When I push the mail through the thin, golden mail-slot, it's suddenly ripped from my hand, and there follows the most unnatural and awful sounds of tearing and ferocious gnawing.

Ah, yes, these are just some of the sweet sounds that fill a typical neighborhood, the sounds a mailman hears day in and day out. It's a beautiful thing, if you're deaf.

In addition to being nuts, all dogs are obsessive compulsive by nature. This is to say, that when they see us coming, they behave nearly the same way each and every day. Some repeatedly slam up against windows with their heads or chests. Some hop up and down, while yet others spin around at great speeds, never showing any signs of dizziness. One dog that I cleverly dubbed "Spinner Dog" was incredibly gifted in this respect. He would run to the door, stop on a dime and start spinning like a class five tornado. Early on while I was still intrigued by the sight, I would take my time near the mailbox, acting as if I were sifting through the mail just so I could see how long he could keep it up. I never saw him tire once. Not even a little.

Some dogs use the line attached to their collar as a tool for rocket propulsion. When they come charging from out of their dog houses they will, just before reaching the end of their line, turn sharply to one side and fly through the air like a tether ball making its circuit. A few are really good at timing their jumps and catch some serious air. Of course the scene isn't complete unless you picture them howling wildly with each lift off.

All of these obsessive compulsive traits are inevitably accompanied by a wide variety of yaps. In the course of my career, I have noted several different categories of yap.

One of the most common and most distinctive comes from the toy dog family- something like a Fox Terrier. Picture the scene. Poking his head out through the slits of a wooden fence is our happy little friend, Mr. Toy Terrier. His tail is wagging hard, tongue shooting out in quick, excited licks, face beaming with joy, clearly overwhelmed with the mailman's arrival. His bark is high pitched and infrequent at first, but as I near, it begins to increase in rapidity, clearly building towards a crescendo.

The inflection and barking pattern communicates something like this: "Hey, look guys, it's the mailman! Whoopee, the mailman! Oh, here he comes. He's getting closer. Closer! Closer!!! He's here! Oh, he's here at last! THIS IS GREAT! Everybody look, the mailman!!!... Wait a minute... Where are you going? No, you can't leave. Get back here. Get back here now! NOW!!! How dare you leave? Oh, I hate you, mailman! I hate you!!! *I loathe you! DIE...*"

Another common type of bark is the "I don't know why I am barking, but I just am" kind of bark. There is usually a long-haired dog sitting out in the middle of its owner's lawn looking blankly around at the sky or trees. Without turning towards me, he lets out a "woof" every now and then. He might actually stand up and meander around, but the whole enterprise is performed without heart or commitment. This one isn't too annoying.

There's also the older dog's obligatory bark. Some old hound dog on a porch will raise an eyebrow, lift his head slightly and let out a slow, very non-threatening, "Ooooorrrrr," and then return to a restful position. It's the, "Master, how about taking a peek out your window, somebody's here" kind of bark.

There are, of course, a multitude of maniacal and angry yaps that could be broken down into sub-categories and explored at length, but for the sake of brevity such nuances will be reduced to a single category. And basically, they communicate one very simple message: "If I could just get my paws on you..." or, "Prepare to meet your Maker, mailman."

While passing by houses with tall privacy fences, some of the most ungodly and terrifying sounds can be heard emanating from hidden and unbalanced dogs. This leaves a lot of room for the imagination to conjure terrible images, for all that can be seen of the animal is a dark outline of something large through the thin slits. I've nearly jumped out of my shoes before when a snout suddenly appears from underneath one of the privacy fences, reaching and snapping at the air, sometimes even chewing on the wood. Passing by in an ever widening arc, the mouth continues to wiggle in rage as it searches for something to latch on to. "I know you're out there, mailman. Come here and let me taste ya!"

Large dogs are especially fond of bashing into things. They smash into front doors, fences, walls, gates, and sometimes even windows. It's rare, but once in a while the truly fanatical will burst out a window and soar through the air like a furry torpedo, sending shards of glass flying in all directions. Often the dog's owner starts cursing wildly, shocked that the glass didn't hold. Imagine that. Who would think that a ninety-pound dog could slam through an old, brittle plate glass window?

I can distinctly remember the solemn warning I once received from Sam Collins, one of the quieter and more subdued carriers at my office, when he found out that I was going to be delivering the mail to this one particularly nasty dog's house; a dog that had successfully jumped through a window in order to devour him.

He said, "Seriously, Austin, this dog is nuts. There are bad dogs, as you well know, but this thing falls into a whole new category. If he's ever loose, you run, ok? Forget the mail and just start running. No, seriously. Run."

When I first encountered this deranged animal, a dark brown grizzly filled with hate and muscle, some kind of Pit Bull-Rottweiler-T-Rex mix, he pounded against the door so hard and with such tremendous force that I genuinely wondered if the bolt would hold.

This dog is crazy! Slam! *You've got to be kidding!* Slam! Slam! *Oh, crap! Run!!!*

Since that initial encounter, I've been "afforded the pleasure" of delivering the mail to his house on many different occasions.

The front yard to the dog's home is a small grassy place, open and treeless. On a slightly crooked sign posted in a window, the following words are written in bold orange letters: "Beware of the Dog." Three cement steps ascend to an enclosed sun porch where, right next to the front door, hangs the mailbox. When I approach, I know he's in there. I fully expect him to jump up and roar, but it doesn't matter. Every time that Behemoth rears up and body slams the door, I nearly wet my pants. And I hate how he glares at me. While pressing his ugly face up against the glass, fogging the window with its hot breath, he turns to the side revealing one dark, hateful eye.

The worst though is when nothing happens. I try to assure myself that the dog is merely deep inside his owner's house, sleeping upstairs, maybe. But then again, maybe he isn't. Maybe he's out back? Maybe he's out back, unchained and free? So after dropping off the mail, I'll warily peer between the houses, expecting to see him rounding the corner, laughing deviously, "Mwa-ha-ha-ha."

Man that dog freaks me out.

It's hard to consider the merits of the leash and not break out in sudden praise. For, oh, what simplicity! Merely hook one end to a dog, and affix the other to a tree, and whalla! one stuck pup. It's truly glorious. And nobody is confused about the function of a leash. It's a leash, a simple rope or section of chain. No complicated instructions. No detailed manuals. No laborious assembly either. The simplest of minds can use it, and because of that, it is one of the greatest inventions in all human history.

And yet there is one profound drawback. The leash is a ticking time bomb.

Few understand this like the mailman. For when Fido barrels out of his dog house, jerking painfully to a sudden stop, body flipping round like a rag doll, yes, the mailman finds this amusing, but he also knows that on a microscopic level, there has just occurred an imperceptible weakening of the restraint. It might be where the rope is attached to the collar. It might be located on the rope itself. Or it might be the metal hook screwed into the ever deteriorating wood. All of these, you see, are potential time bombs. For as the rain continues to beat down, ever so slowly wearing the material away, and as the dog continues to jerk against the restraint, pulling it, twisting it, gnawing on it, the mailman knows his time is short. He can imagine the fibers stretching, tearing; he sees the very molecules pulling apart.

Day after day, I walk by crazed dogs on leashes like this, cracking their necks, fueling their rage by filling storehouses of frustration with daily injury.

Terrible is that moment when the leash finally snaps.

Weeks and weeks, maybe months, even years, of pent up hatred are suddenly unleashed on the mailman, when that once glorious line fails.

I can still remember the day when Harley, a one hundred and thirty-pound Rottweiler, a dog of truly awesome strength, snapped his log chain (Yes, log chain). Normally, the dog would merely leap up and down and tug against the inch thick steel from a safe distance, and I wouldn't pay him much attention. But when I heard the sound of hard breathing only a few feet away, I looked up, and to my utter horror saw him standing beside me, muscles rippling in the afternoon light, neck thick and sweaty with a long section of log chain slithering on the ground behind him.

Amazingly, he spared my life, watching me slowly crawl away in a fetal position. Most dogs would have gone for the kill. My only guess is that since Amy was his master, a window clerk at my office, he must have figured killing one of her coworkers would be frowned upon.

So, anyway, the leash has its distinct limitations.

Now listen. The leash is still great. Easily a 9 out of 10. But if you want to talk about the crème de la crème, a real work of art, then we have to talk about the Shock Collar. I have no idea who invented this thing, but they seriously deserve the Nobel Peace Prize. It's incredible. Here's how it works. Each time a dog wearing the special device barks, the collar sends out a low voltage zap, thus "deterring undesirable behavior," to use the language of advertisers. How's that for technology? Fido sees the mailman, starts barking his guts out, and ZAP! Electric love, baby.

It's obvious when a dog is trying to acclimate to the equipment. He will bark, pause, and show signs of concern, tilting his head curiously. He barks again, yelps, and then looks around in confusion, "What the! Who did that?" On and on it goes until he finally learns to connect barking with discomfort. When he figures that out, life isn't so bad. But it's a hard lesson to learn when the mailman comes around. It can take weeks before Fido learns to keep quiet. Of course, this is made exceedingly difficult when the mailman continues to egg the dog on by making sudden, semi-aggressive movements like stomping his foot or faking a lunge. But you know we would never do that.

Chapter 5

Frolicking in the Snow

"Winter either bites with its teeth or lashes with its tail."

-Unknown-

———————————

On that bitterly cold, January morning, while turning my head from side to side trying desperately to shield my face from the howling winds, I thought to myself, *Oh, why didn't I listen to Whaleman?*

Earlier in the day, back in the men's locker room at the Post Office, while Frank Whaleman was zipping up his jacket, preparing himself for one of the year's coldest days, he called out in a loud voice, "You'd better put on everything you've got, Brownie."

"Oh, you think so?" I said with a measure of concern. "But is that all you're going to wear?"

Whaleman laughed and shook his bushy head, his untamed beard following each shake. "You see this right here?" he said patting his immense girth- a girth befitting that of a Norwegian Viking. "This is R-40 insulation. I've got built in winter clothes, man." He laughed harder.

I looked down at my tall, 145 pound-when-wet-frame and didn't see anything even slightly resembling R-40 insulation. I didn't see anything resembling R-2.5 insulation for that matter. I looked more like Scooby Doo's side kick, Shaggy, than someone descending from Scandinavian stock.

I turned back to my locker and looked over the gear I had. There were a pair of galoshes, some hill-jack looking long underwear, a black sock cap, some knitted gloves with little rubber dots all over them, a wadded up T-shirt, a sweatshirt and a lightweight jacket. That seemed good enough. I'd just put on the long underwear, throw on the sweatshirt, zip up my jacket and crown my head with a black sock cap. I was good to go.

Now it must be understood that we carriers receive something called a clothing allotment. Each year, ninety days after our hire-in-date, we are given a modest chunk of change to purchase postal gear. The figure has gone up over the years, but when I first started the allowance was about 300 dollars. That might sound substantial, but there's a catch. There are only a handful of companies that sell postal attire and they want you to believe that a medium-weight trouser is worth fifty bucks. In addition to that, a pair of shoes runs eighty dollars. A windbreaker costs fifty-five dollars, and something a little more substantial like a men's bomber jacket tickles the hundred dollar mark. So let's see, two pair of pants, one pair of shorts, one pair of shoes, two shirts and a windbreaker comes out to around 290 big ones. Ye haw! Throw in a belt and cap and you're ready for ten rounds with Jack Frost. Right.

Since this was my first winter as a mailman, it goes without saying that most of the gear I possessed was junk that I found in my winter closet, the one that's piled up with old boots, single gloves and a general heap of mismatched winter paraphernalia all tangled together into a cemetery of forgotten clothes. I don't know if it was simply a failure to think things through or if it was genuine stupidity, but I actually felt confident that my knitted gloves- gloves that revealed tiny patches of pink skin between each knit- were sufficient for wind chills exceeding negative forty. Either way, I was a moron.

So there I was on 4th street, not more than five minutes into my first relay, wondering if I might actually be the first carrier to die of exposure while walking with the mail. I had been cold before, but nothing had come even remotely close to this.

It's been said that dying from hypothermia is a pretty descent way to go overall. At first you're cold and shiver, but then you get kind of drowsy, and after that you just lie down and go to sleep. Well listen, whoever thinks that is wrong. They are very, very wrong. While it's true that I didn't quite make it to that snuggly state of hypothermic bliss- maybe that was just around the corner- everything leading up to that sanguine moment felt exceedingly unpleasant. Imagine being repeatedly kicked in the privates by Frosty the Snowman. That's the general sensation.

About half-way through the relay, I leaned up against one of our downtown buildings. I was genuinely afraid. Images of black noses, chipped ears and missing appendages filled my thoughts. I could almost hear the grim voice of my old health and safety teacher describing the symptoms of frostbite, "Frostbite is usually marked by discoloration of the skin, along with burning or tingling sensations, partial or complete numbness and possibly intense pain." I took my gloves off to consider my hands. That's when I noticed that my nose felt strangely absent.

What am I going to do? I thought to myself. One thing was very clear; I couldn't keep going on like this. But I couldn't go back to the post office either. The thought of going back felt shameful, somehow dishonorable. Thousands of other mailmen were trudging through similar conditions and faithfully persevering. And besides, management would simply tell me, "Cold? Just go faster. That'll warm ya up."

I slipped my gloves back on and set off again.

Towards the end of the relay, I entered a smoky tavern. Several local heads turned my direction. The bartender stopped wiping down a glass. He stared at me for a moment and then asked, "Stay'in warm enough, mailman?"

There was a time when a mailman would have happily accepted a shot of something strong to warm his limbs. But now drinking isn't allowed. Regardless, I wasn't even twenty years old yet, so I simply shook my head, set down the mail and stumbled back out into the cold.

When I reached my truck, I had to find more clothes and fast. There wasn't anything back at the post office, so the only option left was to go home and try to dig up something. So that's what I did. I took an extremely early lunch break in order to find something that I knew didn't exist. Brilliant.

My wife came home from canceled classes to find her wild eyed husband frantically searching for something warm to wear. There were clothes scattered everywhere, and I was kneeling down in the middle of the mess murmuring strange things.

"What's wrong?" Bek asked with a concerned look.

At that point it would have been convenient for me to hold up some missing fingers, but I wasn't quite to that point, so I explained my dire situation to her, accentuating the fact that I desperately needed good boots, good gloves, a warmer coat and a face mask; basically, I needed everything.

She looked down at the floor and said, "I don't think we have much."

I dropped an orange mitten and welcomed despair. Everything seemed hopeless. Time was slipping away and my options were dwindling fast. Would I join the Postal Hall of Shame and give up or consign myself to death by exposure?

An idea came to me. I wondered if my parents, who lived fairly close by, might have anything I could use in their forgotten stash of winter clothes. And so I picked up the phone, gave a lugubrious account of my misfortunes to my Mom and smiled when she said, "I think I might have a few things that could work. I'll be right over."

Fifteen minutes later, my mom came in carrying an armful of winter gear. My brows furrowed with strange curiosity when she unrolled a bright, and I mean bright, red snowmobile suit (something which would later be affectionately known as "Big Red.") It had to be at least 63 color steps from postal blue, but it looked like it could handle the frigid temperatures of deep space. Some thick gloves hit the ground as well as an equally bright, orange face mask. Lastly, there was a pair of moon boots that had something like a rainbow wrapped around them. They screamed 1981.

"These will keep you warm," she reassured me.

My wife was smiling. I just stared at the equipment.

There's an old saying that goes something like this: beggars can't be choosers. At that moment I was the most desperate of all beggars and would have been willing to wear a "My Little Pony" outfit if it would only keep me warm, so I picked up the snowsuit and began working my way into it.

As a child there would have been an exhilarating sense of excitement to this whole zipping and strapping and tugging process, an anticipation of snowy things, like building forts, sliding down hills, throwing snowballs, but at that moment, while sitting on the floor, pulling on those moon boots and donning my head with a bright ski mask, the infinite gaiety of youthful bliss somehow escaped my notice.

Struggling to my feet, I stood and brushed some dust off my chest. Turning, I presented myself to my onlookers. They were grinning real hard. While obviously holding back laughter, my Mom finally said, "That'll definitely keep you warm."

Sure, I was going to be the first walking light saber in postal history, but I really didn't care. I could take a comfortable nap on Pluto with the outfit I had on, and that made me supremely happy.

When I returned to the route, I felt all warm and toasty. My hands didn't hurt, I could feel my feet and my face felt snuggly. My pride had taken a serious hit that day, and I received a number of funny expressions from children as they watched me pass by their window, sometimes screaming out, "Look, Mommy! Look!" But that didn't faze me too much, for I was back up again and Jack Frost's jabs and right hooks were being easily deflected by good old Big Red. The route would be finished.

There's a scene in the movie *Cast Away* where Tom Hanks is standing on a rock amid the surf with an air of manliness and skill, his body tan and lean with muscle. His expression is serious and controlled as a spear slices through the water and nails a fish twenty feet away. Picking it up, he casually begins eating it raw, without the slightest hint of revulsion. Having spent many weeks on the island, the once soft and unfit character is transformed into an adept survivalist capable of handling the challenges of the island.

In some remote and vague sense, that scene illustrates the similar transformation that has taken place in my own life over the years. Don't get me wrong. I am far, far away from joining the polar bear club, and winter still has a suck factor of ten, but I have grown more accustomed to handling the erratic and sometimes extreme conditions Indiana weather can dish out. Maybe it would be better to say that I've simply been able to accumulate better equipment over the years. I've retired Big Red into the Hall of Fame and picked up in its place some pretty snazzy ski pants. The cheaply knit gloves are gone, and I now own a black pair of rugged

Manzellas, gloves boasting forty grams of Thinsulate. My moon boots, as well as a host of other clunky or heavy or extremely uncomfortable, rub-the-back-of-my-heels-to-the-bone snow shoes, have been tossed out for the incredibly lightweight and warm Neos Explorers. But let me stress again, even if a mailman has the best gear known to mankind, the 007 specials, winter is still perfectly capable of kicking his butt.

Unfortunately, winter has probably been most traumatic for my mother. It would seem that the days of Big Red have left an indelible impression of the tempest's fury on her mind. Her "little boy" was "nearly decimated" by Jack Frost and this has had the effect of elevating an already innate desire to protect her offspring to monumental heights.

I'll be sitting in my living room stretched out on the couch and the phone will ring.

"Hello. Hi, Mom. They're predicting snow six days from now? Oh, yeah. Wow, that bad, huh? Really... uhuh...uhuh... Yeah, I'll have my polypropylene long underwear. No, no, I'm good to go. I'll be careful. Ok, I'll keep a watch out. Ok, see ya. Bye. "

I can usually look forward to receiving several pairs of the thickest, warmest socks that Greenland's finest can handcraft as a Christmas present each year. Besides a genuine appreciation for good socks, I find her motherly concerns endearing. It's always good to know that someone is praying for you when it starts snowing.

I'm tempted to say that some of my mother's zeal is spurred on by the behavior of local newscasters. Is it just me or do those guys get all worked up into a lather at even the remotest possibility of inclement weather? I'll be watching the news, listening to them talk about the latest issues, when suddenly their voices take on a new, more serious tone when they come to the local forecast. It's as if their whole countenance changes as something like an apocalyptic fervor enters their soul. And as they talk about the potential dangers of bad weather, a foreboding sense of death is mixed with an element of restrained ecstasy. I'm not sure, but I have a deep suspicion that when the meteorologist walks into the room and tells the broadcasters that there's a chance of a winter storm, they nod their heads in a kind of "Yes! Yes!" and give each other high fives.

"This is our moment to shine! The whole listening area is looking to us to guide them through the impending chaos..."

It's "Newscasters Gone Wild" if we actually get a decent amount of snowfall. As I write this, we recently had a blizzard blast through our region, and the newscasters had a heyday with the whole affair. "February Fury" was the battle cry. There was some reporter out by a highway shouting excitedly over the wind, "It's bad out here, Dan, real bad. We've got jack-knifed semis and cars in ditches all over the place." The people behind the desk listened with solemn expressions as the brave reporter continued, "The snow is coming down fast, two inches an hour, with no indication of it letting up. It's crazy out here, I tell ya, *crazy!*" He then lifted up something like a piece of cardboard to demonstrate just how hard the wind was blowing. It whipped around as he fought to hold it up for the camera. The brave soul concluded the report and sent it back to the news desk where two anchors exchanged looks of astonishment and then, in a doomsday kind of voice, warned us about the coming end of the world.

Don't get me wrong, the weather was pretty bad for a couple of days during "February Fury," but it just seems like these folks find some kind of perverted pleasure in things like "icy roads" and "dangerous conditions." All of this isn't good for my mother's heart, and it usually means that we mailmen will hear, oh, about 2000 weather reports out on the route, sometimes in the same "We're all gonna die" tone. It's for this reason that I usually try to avoid watching the weather forecast. I'm pretty sure that most mailmen function the same way. What we usually do is stand around the time clock and mutter things like, "It's going to be fun today," or, "Why didn't the supervisor bring us in earlier?" or, "You had better put on everything you've got today, Brownie."

Ironically, those of us who have to actually spend the most time out in the weather talk the least about it. We usually grunt and snort around when things are bad, but rarely do we discuss the weather forecast in any kind of detail, let alone relish it. At the end of the day it really doesn't matter. We're going to be playing outside regardless of what the weather may or may not do.

Walking the mail in the winter is a pretty unique experience overall. In our modern society one would think it strange that someone would actually have to tromp through the snow for miles in order to deliver Victoria Secret catalogs and Wal-Mart fliers. But we do. Sure, there are road crews, crossing guards and a variety of other professions that require outdoor work, but for the most part the mailman is the only one who really gets close and personal with winter for long periods of time. The trash man may very well have it as bad, or worse, than we do, but it's hard to tell, for just about the time I get to know one of them well enough to begin trading stories, they get whisked off to prison. So anyway, I'm going to assume that waste management is in the running. At any rate, I feel pretty confident that we mailmen experience a lot of things that most people just don't have the luxury of experiencing.

If anyone can relate to our job, it's got to be mountaineers. In this respect, I have wondered how similar our wintery travails compare with something like climbing Mount Everest. They definitely have us on elevation, but I'm yet to see a picture of one of those guys trying to finger the mail while making their ascent. Moreover, we've only got one free hand, while they've got two. And good luck sorting through the mail with those thick gloves~ it would be like an ogre trying to thread a needle with those things. Let's call their icy crevasses a wash in light of our slippery, unshoveled steps. Their temperatures are certainly more extreme, but last time I checked they don't have to worry about dogs up there. They carry heavy packs, we have our mail satchels. They have base camps, we have Wendy's. Their summit is equivalent to our driving relays and, this is a big one, climbing Mount Everest is esteemed as a once in a lifetime achievement worthy of praise. We come crawling back to the Post Office only to be greeted by management, hands on hips, grunting, "What took you so long?"

There's definitely one thing that you won't see up on Mount Everest and that's an eighty year old woman trying to shovel her walk. It's the darndest thing. You can have a house full of college athletes asking, "Snow shovel? What's that?" but little ol' Mrs. Jones will be outside laboring away at her steps for three hours in her nightgown. I can't understand it. No, seriously, more often than not, there will be an elderly man on the verge of coronary failure, faithfully shoveling away at his sidewalk, while Billy plays his X-Box all day while stretched out on the couch. There's a moral to be preached at this juncture, but I'll refrain. Just remember to help out your elders, Billy, ok?

All in all, winter's tough. It can be crazy tough. But here's the thing. Not all carriers hate winter. In fact, some actually like it. Actually prefer it. And this boggles my mind.

Take Frank Whaleman, the guy with the R-40 insulation. He loves cold weather. The guy walks around in a short sleeve shirt when it's thirty degrees. And it isn't a macho thing either. He's like one of those husky dogs that love to roll around with their face in the snow. The cold simply doesn't bother him. And then there's Jake Bardillion, a pot-bellied, bearded man with slicked back hair, who is, by all accounts, a freak of nature. It can be negative eight with twenty mile-an-hour winds and the guy walks around with a windbreaker on. No hat. Maybe gloves. And under his jacket, only a long sleeved shirt. While I'm waddling around the parking lot loading up my truck, looking like a bloated tick because of the thirteen layers under my parka, he's standing at the rear door of his truck smiling, sucking in the frigid air. Then he looks over at me. "What's wrong with you, Brownie? You act like it's cold out here."

"Cold? It's *freaking freezing.*"

"Ah, come on, you weenie. It's not cold out here. It's just right."

He's serious.

But when July rolls around, Bardillion looks like a dying man. Sweating. Suffering. Puking. Crawling. Gatorade IV. The man barely survives summer.

So when it comes to handling the cold, Jake Bardillion is a juggernaut. But the man who takes the prize would have to be Vincent Scholl. Only recently did I hear about him. Leon Morris recounted the story one early morning in January. A group of about six carriers were standing in the middle of the workroom floor in near complete darkness. I was one of the six. A heinous ice storm had just rolled through, knocking ninety-five percent of the power out of our city. Our post office was no exception. And the emergency lights failed. So there we stood, huddled together, six shadowy forms, listening to Leon talk about the storm of seventy-eight and the man, Vincent Scholl.

"The blizzard of seventy-eight. It was the worst storm in thirty years of walking the mail. Twenty-foot snow drifts. Howling winds. It was easily negative sixty."

Two other older carriers grunted in agreement.

"I'd say more like negative seventy," One amended.

"*Negative seventy?*" I blurted out.

"Easily. Austin, let me tell ya, it was BE-YOND cold."

"So why in the world did the Postmaster send you out? That's nuts."

"He told us to do what we could. So we packed up and headed out. Loady over there (Leon pointed to a guy nicknamed "The Load" because he once had an accident in his shorts after eating something disagreeable) came back only fifteen minutes later. The Postmaster met him at the door, 'What the heck you doing back already?' And Loady said, 'It's cold out there." "You gotta give it more than fifteen minutes, Load.' So out went Loady again. During this time, I was walking over on North Street. Going east wasn't too bad. But west was a bear. Right into the wind. Nothing could keep you warm. I mean nothing. So after my first relay, I stopped in at Steve's Pub and downed a couple shots. Then I set off again. I'm out there on my second relay when here comes the Postmaster in his truck. He rolls down the window and says, 'Look. It's just too bad out here. Go ahead and finish off this relay and head on back.' I tell him, 'Like hell. I'm riding back with you.' So he gave me a ride back. After that, he and another manager went looking around for the other carriers. But they couldn't find Vincent. Now there's something about Vincent you need to know. The man never wore gloves. Never. He hated the things. Said he couldn't move his fingers. I don't even think he owned a pair."

I interrupted. "Are you telling me he went out in negative-seventy degree temperatures without gloves?"

"Yup."

Leon explained, "The guy was as tough as nails. He served in World War II. My guess is that in Bastogne he experienced a cold we'll never understand."

After a moment's silence, he continued, "So there's the supervisor and the Postmaster searching all over for Vincent. Come to find out, Vincent saw them from a distance and hid. He knew they wanted him to return back to the office. But he wanted to finish the rounds. So every time they'd come around the corner, he'd jump behind a car or hide near a house. They never did find him."

"So he finished the route?"

"He did."

Let's not forget one other thing. There are plenty of mailmen who go all year without ever slipping on a pair of gloves or wearing long underwear. Of course, this isn't because they're made of the same stuff as Vincent Scholl. Quite the contrary. They're totally silky. And that's because they don't have to deal with winter, because, of course, they live in states where things don't get hairy during the month of January. Oh, sure, they might have to put on a sweater, but a parka? Not in Florida. Not in most of Arizona. Good grief, not in Hawaii.

Naturally, I'm just jealous, for I'd love nothing more than to be a pansy just like them. I actually begin to quiver with joy at the mere thought of wearing shorts year round, of seeing the sun during the month of February, of ditching my ski pants and burning my face mask. I can't imagine it. It feels impossibly distant. That's why I'm rooting for global warming. Sure, there's been a lot of talk, mostly negative talk about it, but I'm still crossing my fingers. People scream, "Look out, we're all gonna die," but frankly, I'm having a hard time seeing the downside. Ok, so a few polar bears get a little sweaty and some ice melts. What's the big deal? Last I checked, people aren't flocking to Iceland. Maybe a little adjustment would do them some good? Maybe their beaches would begin to boom?

Yeah, well I suppose it's out of my hands. Ever since the government banned fluorocarbons in aerosol spray cans, there's not much I can do.

But there is another option. There is one other hope for mailmen like myself. And that hope is summed up in one very special word.

Transfer.

The word is "Transfer."

In the postal system there's a way for mailmen to escape the shackles of winter, and that's to successfully find the key of mutual exchange and trade spots with another carrier. But this key, of which we shall speak about in a later chapter, is an elusive key, and one few ever find. But for those who do find it, they are afforded many, many warm pleasures.

Chapter 6

Porcelain Sanctuaries

"Today, the degradation of the inner life is symbolized by the fact that the only place sacred from interruption is the private toilet."

-Louis Mumford-

"There is only one immutable law in life- in a gentleman's toilet, incoming traffic has the right of way."

-Hugh Leonard-

––––––––––––––––––––

So you're hiking with your friends in the woods, enjoying nature, laughing about old times, when you feel a slight gurgle somewhere deep within your lower regions. A wee little expression of concern forms on your face, but while brushing away a low hanging branch, you shrug it off and continue on. As the path begins to meander up a hill, you notice another gurgle, though now it's a little more pronounced, and it's soon followed by that all too familiar feeling.

Uh, oh, you think to yourself, as you slacken your pace. One very clear and poignant thought rings out in your mind, *Bathroom! Where's a bathroom?*

We've all been there before. Whether it's on a trail or on the interstate or in an important board meeting, we've all felt that foreboding gurgle. It's not a good feeling. Fortunately, for many of us, the red siren doesn't go off while we're geographically challenged; a bathroom is usually a hop, skip and a jump away-sometimes literally! But for the mailman, this is a serious concern, a relay-by-relay concern, mind you.

It's a little known fact that letter carriers strategically plan out their line of retreat to a bathroom. Every potential latrine within a three mile radius has been scoped out and pondered at length. We know how long it takes to get there. We know its condition. We know how popular it is. We know how well stocked it is. It is a universal truth that all mailmen covet well ordered bathrooms. We absolutely adore a centrally located toilet. And we rejoice all the more if it has one of those little air fresheners in it. You may not know it, those of you working at a business, but your commode just might be a mailman's golden spot; a water hole in a desert; a porcelain sanctuary.

But for every sparkling toilet, there are a dozen bad ones. And this troubles the mailman. Good bathrooms are hard to come by; they're an endangered species. But I'm not telling you anything new, am I? I know you've taken your dancing little Timmy to the back of Wal-Mart only to be instantly vaporized by an unearthly odor when you open the door. We've all gone into a mall restroom and pondered how we might accomplish the task without touching anything. And I certainly know that you are well aware of the state of bathrooms at gas stations. They're legendary. You swing open the door and look in horror at what lies before you. A bare bulb flickers with electrical excitement, the floor is littered with used paper towels, the dripping sink has grimy splotches all over it, and the toilet is at flood level with water swirling ever so slowly.

Yep, like I said, a good bathroom should be cherished, because they are few and far between.

I suppose someone may want to know if privately owned toilets are available to mailmen and if they're a good option. Well, homeowners on the route have offered their bathrooms to me before, but it's not too often that a carrier feels buddy-buddy enough with the people to actually go through with it. I might venture a tinkle if I know them really well, but do you really want to drop off a parcel in their home? You've gotta be real tight with the folks to do that. For myself, I'd much rather make a run for the border and use Taco Bell's bathroom. I'm pretty sure that this is the general consensus among mailmen.

Now there are four categories by which all bathrooms are judged. We consider their traffic volumes, their cleanliness, the aroma factor and accessibility. If a bathroom hopes to attain high marks, they have to nail down at least three of these categories. It's hard to say which is the most important, but traffic is right up there in my estimation.

Allow me to paint a picture. You're right in the middle of a relay when suddenly the call of nature comes knocking. Unless it's an emergency, you aren't going to high tail it back to the truck, so you finish off the relay and zip off for the nearest restroom. When the light up ahead turns red, you give the steering wheel a "whack!" And as you wait out the signal, your left leg begins to bounce impatiently up and down.

"Come on..." you mutter. "Come on..."

"Oh, come on!" you say, as a little old lady hesitates to go when the light turns green.

Zooming down the road, you make a sharp turn into the McDonald's parking lot, jump out of the truck, lock it, and scurry off towards the front door. You can't help but feel like everyone's staring at you as you proceed to walk in a slightly unnatural and uneasy manner towards the bathroom door. Your eyes widen as right before you an old man stands up from a table and enters the bathroom with a newspaper tucked under his arm.

Maybe he's just going to wash his hands, you think, knowing better.

When you push your way in to the restroom, you just catch the soft sound of the latch sliding shut on the stall door. Naturally, there's only one stall.

Needless to say, traffic levels are absolutely crucial in a pinch. The last thing you want to do when things are urgent is wait around for Old Man Tucker to finish reading the sports section. So when we mailmen consider the various bathrooms available to us, traffic volume and capacity are very important factors in the equation.

Solitude is significant also. If there's one thing that can shatter your peace in an instant, it's a jiggling door handle.

Loudly, "Mommy! The door's locked! I can't get in!" Jiggle, jiggle jiggle...

A couple seconds go by.

Quieter, "Mommy, I can't open it."

In a soft voice, "Honey, there's someone in there, just be patient..."

Serenity gone.

Nobody likes to be rushed, and the restroom is no exception. A mailman wants to take his time and get off his feet. He wants to relax and enjoy the break. There might also be a lot of gear to shed for the event, which is annoying enough without having to listen to little Johnny bang on the door.

So that's the traffic factor. Now let's talk about a related issue, namely, the aroma factor. And for this, I've got to share a story.

In my town, there's a fast food joint called the Burger Barn. It's a decent little restaurant. One of their strong points is a wide selection of food. You can order chicken, burgers, various soups, mashed potatoes, grilled ham and a host of other tasty things. The decorum leaves a bit to be desired, but what does someone expect from a place called the Burger Barn?

I might talk about this at greater length elsewhere, but you need to understand that I have some rather odd eating habits. If I can, I will eat at the same place every day. I like the familiarity of it all. If there's something on the menu that jazzes me, then I'll get that exact same thing for months, even years, until I'm thoroughly sick of it. I know, it's kind of strange, but that's what I do.

Anyway, there's this farmer looking guy who swings by to chat with the ladies behind the counter. He often hangs around for twenty or thirty minutes and talks about whatever farmers talk about. Reading between the lines, I'm guessing that he supplies the restaurant with meat.

I can still remember the first couple of times when I ventured off to wash my hands only to realize that the single occupancy restroom was locked. I stood there and waited, and waited, and waited, gave up, went back to the register, picked up my order, got my condiments, sat down at a seat where I could still see the hallway leading to the bathroom and cocked my head in growing curiosity as time after time it seemed to be this same farmer guy preventing me from washing my hands.

While chewing on a fry, I watched him leisurely walk out of the bathroom, hands tugging at the waistline in attempt to get his pants just right.

Hmmm...

Rising slowly, I made my way for the bathroom. Pausing at the door for a second, I braced myself for what might follow. With a sudden push, I entered.

The smell that filled that little room defies description. No seriously, it was so bad that I genuinely wondered if it could be hazardous to my health. I thought I might black out. And since there was a vent in the ceiling gushing out hot air into the cramped quarters, it only intensified the feeling of suffocation.

It was truly amazing how this same scenario would occur day after day. I could get there twenty minutes earlier or twenty minutes later to no purpose. Farmer boy would still be in there cooking up his own foul brew.

After awhile, I became impressed with my ability to hold my breath for long periods of time. I've heard that free-divers have incredible lung capacities and can withstand the crushing depths of the ocean for several minutes. I fancied that Burger Barn was preparing me for the open waters, for I eventually got to a point where I could enter the restroom, go to the bathroom and wash my hands all on one breath of air. Bad smell or no smell, I never knew for sure, for I always preemptively hyperventilated a few times, sucked in one last gulp of air, held it and casually went about my business. This technique worked well enough, but is this how one really wants to function? I mean seriously, isn't there a better way?

So I trust that you can now more fully appreciate the intimate connection between a high traffic bathroom and the aroma factor. The two go hand in hand, for the former entails the latter.

And so the mailman yearns for an isolated, clean, nearby bathroom. These are rare, however, very, very rare. But in my own travels, I have found one secret place that surpasses all other locations. It's so secretive in fact, that, so far as I know, I and only one other mailman know about this spot. It is as clean and untouched as the distant peaks of a far away land. The air is fresh and scented with something peachy. The tiles sparkle and gleam under the soft rays of inset lighting. The soap is filled to the top and there's an endless supply of paper towels. It's a dream spot. And it's all my own. I have searched for years for such a bathroom, and I have found it. Once you learn where it's located, you'll understand why it's so perfect.

Ready?

It is the men's restroom at the women's clinic.

Yep, that's right. Just let that soak in for a moment. The men's restroom at the women's clinic. Could there be a more ideal location? And since this particular clinic has been added recently to our hospital, everything's new and modern. I walk in through automatic sliding doors, angle to my left across a tiled floor and "Voila!" the men's restroom. I'm almost getting misty eyed just thinking about it.

I'll confidently stride in through the swinging door, without the slightest fear that stall number one is occupied. And I'll take my sweet time, not the least bit concerned of interruption. I dare say that a nuclear bomb could be dropped in our downtown area without my noticing it in this tranquil place.

All is quiet and serene.

All was quiet and serene, that is, until one day I walked in and noticed one of those mobile janitor stations positioned in front of the entrance, the ones on wheels that have a tangled array of spray bottles and squeegees hanging from them.

Hey, what's this?

My confident stride was cut short when I opened the door and met a middle-aged man in a janitor's uniform wiping down the countertops around the sink area.

"Hello, there," said the janitor, with a friendly tone.

"Oh, hi."

"So how's walkin the mail these days?" He asked.

"It's, uh, it's-it's good."

"Good, good. So..." and then the man began to chat with me during the whole of my bathroom experience. He was a nice guy, someone I might even invite over for poker night, but his presence still dampened my mood. Oh, well. What's one friendly chat anyway? But it didn't prove to be merely one friendly chat. All too often I would walk in through those automatic doors only to see the janitor station parked outside the restroom entrance with one of those "Slippery when wet" signs propped up in front of it.

Oh, come on. What's up with this?

Then it occurred to me. Maybe this guy liked the solitude of the bathroom as much as I did. Maybe he too found the spot to be a sanctuary from the outside world. Could I blame him? But what was I going to do? Something had to give.

I walked in just as he was coming out.

"It's all yours," he said with a smile.

All mine? It wasn't his to give, right? I felt panicked. The world was crumbling all around me. I had to do something.

As I entered and stood inside, pondering the depths of the unfolding injustice, the swinging door shut and revealed a white piece of paper attached to the door. The paper was enclosed in a clear, plastic sleeve and had markings on it. Curiosity drew me in close. It appeared to be a kind of register log. There was a place for a signature, the date and time. And there must have been at least eleven or twelve blanks filled by the hands of two different men. I scanned down the list.

Four days ago, at 11:30 am, John.

Three days ago, 3:40 pm, Bill.

Two days ago, 3:45 pm, John.

At the end the following inscription read: 3:38 pm, Bill, with the current date.

Glancing down at my watch, it read 3:40 pm.

Joy reentered my soul as I realized that there was a pattern to the cleanings. I felt all at once like a general who had learned of his enemy's position. Now I could anticipate their movements, dodge them at will. I could observe any changes in their behavior and adjust accordingly.

And so all was well once again, for I had regained the bliss of having the perfect bathroom all to myself, its rightful owner.

Chapter 7

Bold Beginnings and Grand Advancements

"In mid-century America, communication between St. Joseph on
the fringe of western settlement and gold mining communities of
California challenged the bold and made skeptical the timid. Into
this picture rode the Pony Express. In rain and in snow, in sleet
and in hail over moonlit prairie, down tortuous mountain path . . .
pounding pony feet knitted together the ragged edges of a rising
nation."

- Frank S. Popplewell-

A hush came over the crowd as the mayor, a Colonel M. Jeff
Thompson, made his way to the front of the group. Eager
spectators leaned and craned their necks in order to gain a better
view of the man. Raising his dignified chin into the air, the mayor
spoke thus:

"My Fellow Citizens:

This is a great day in the history of Saint Joseph. For more
than a decade she has been the portal through which passed the
trains for the great west; the source from which those hardy spirits
who are braving the desert's hardships have drawn their material
and spiritual supplies. Now she is to become the connecting link
between the extremes of the continents; to take up the thread of
telegraphic communication where it was dropped and send it on to
those isolated districts which so eagerly and wistfully await
communications with the great world.

For the first time in the history of America, mail will go by an overland route from the east to the west; in a few hours the first rider in this epoch-making journey will set forth."

On that April evening, the third to be exact, in the year 1860, Mayor Thompson marked the beginning of that seminal, American project, the Pony Express. This bold enterprise has captured the imagination of Americans and has served as a symbol of our country's indomitable spirit and progressive vision.

There's something awe-inspiring about the thought of a lone rider galloping off into the wilderness with the sole intent of delivering a message to someone hundreds of miles away. I like to imagine what it must have felt like to be that first rider who left with the cheers and shouts of the people of St. Joseph spurring him on. They say that he was a Mr. Richardson, a man described by the *The Weekly West* as someone "accustomed to every description of hardship, having sailed for years amid the snows and icebergs of the Northern Ocean." He would be the one to sprint through the first leg of the great journey, a forty-mile run straight into the Wild West. In the cool of the night air, others would be ready to receive the mail pouch, called a *mochila*, and continue along the express line through some six states. The *Sacramento Daily Union*, dated April 14, 1860, recorded the arrival of Sam Williamson, the last rider in the long chain of carriers. There were women on balconies waving their handkerchiefs, heads hanging out windows shouting great hoops of joy, and children on rooftops waving their arms with excitement. There was the blast of a canon followed by a chorus of rifles. Banners reading "Pony Express, Forever' and "Hurrah for the Pony Express" hung proudly in the California streets. Even a cavalcade escorted the Express rider into the town, a charging figure bearing a flag leading the excited procession. And then, in the words of the newspaper, "out of this confounded confusion, mingled fun and earnestness... emerged at last the Pony Express, trotting up to the door of the agency (Alta Telegraph office) and depositing its precious mail in ten days from St. Joseph to Sacramento. Hip, hip, hurrah for the Pony carrier!"

What a magnificent beginning. But even more amazing than all the festivity was the operation itself. Various stops out in the remote wilderness (150 to 190 of them) served as stations for these riders. They would push their horse hard for ten to fifteen miles and then make a switch, jumping on the back of a fresh horse in order to speed off again into the vast western landscape. A single rider typically covered 75-100 miles before calling it a day.

It was certainly a harrowing profession. Adolph Sutro, writing in the Daily Alta Calinfornian, recounts the blizzard-like conditions that met his party of eight while traveling west. He described how the blowing snow felt like needles pelting his face, and how the pine trees creaked and groaned in the howling winds, producing within them an acute fear. When they reached the summit, and thus their shelter, a place called the Strawberry Valley House, they looked out and saw "a lonely rider dashing along at a tremendous rate. We wondered what could possibly induce him to go on through that gale, and thought it must be some important business. It was the Pony Express."

In addition to their having to constantly battle the elements, a dizzying array of other potential hazards ever loomed before them- wild animals, bandits, hostile Indians. All of these could be waiting around the next bend. And let's not forget that in times of trouble they couldn't whip out a cell phone and call for help.

But that's what a gun's for, right? It's hard to believe, but Express riders weren't permitted to carry any weapons. Since strict weight limits had to be adhered to, they traveled unarmed. The rider couldn't weigh more than 125 pounds, and he would usually have 40 pounds of mail and goods bringing him right to the 165-pound weight limit. I think I'd figure out a way to make room for a Winchester, or at least a bowie knife, somehow.

The riders at that weight were obviously small, and so they were often quite young. In fact, the average age of an Express rider hovered around the twenty year mark, the youngest being a mere eleven. Eleven years old! How about it, Mom? Ready to send off your son into the night, all alone, without so much as a slingshot for protection? Given these extreme conditions, it's been reported that the Pony Express looked for orphans to accomplish the dangerous task. Here's how one poster made its appeal:

"Wanted: Young, skinny, wiry fellows not over eighteen. Must be expert riders, willing to risk death daily. Orphans preferred. Wages 25$ per week. Apply Pony Express Stables."

My how things have changed.

Clearly these young men were made of beef jerky or bark. They probably grew up playing with rattle snakes and bears, maybe even those lawn darts that kids tossed around for a while before somebody realized that throwing steel spikes up in the air was a really, really bad idea.

There's no doubt about it, these guys were tough and rugged, courageous and willing to look death right in the face without blinking. But for twenty-five bucks a week, which was awesome money back then, they were willing to take the risk.

Mail delivery in our day and age isn't quite so daring. In fact, one can't help but chuckle at what can only be described as a hyperactive zeal for safety. Allow me to illustrate.

Some time ago, management gathered us together to show us how to properly attach these cleat-like things to our shoes, a product designed to help reduce the chance of slipping on ice. As we sat watching the supervisor demonstrate how to fasten the contraption to our postal approved sneakers, I picked up one of the packages and read the warning label. It said, and I quote:

"Grip-Walker is an aggressive ice walking device and is not intended for indoor use. Grip-Walker is an aide in the prevention of slips and falls, and not a guarantee. Always use utmost caution when walking in potentially slippery areas. Serious injury or death may occur from misuse."

Serious injury or death may occur from misuse? Good heavens! We're talking about foot gear, right?

On another occasion, we were called to the center of the workroom floor to be shown how to properly lift a parcel. There, in the middle of a ring of snickering carriers, the Postmaster squatted, his back straight and rigid, rear arcing prominently, exhibiting a perfect parcel lift. It was a beautiful thing to witness. He successfully lifted the package high into the air. I can just see the Express riders applauding such feats of ergonomic splendor.

There are also innumerable signs scattered around our Post Office warning employees about every potential hazard conceivable to the human mind. There are posters of people suffering from heat stroke; carriers walking carefully on ice; there are mottos detailing good driving habits; videos calling for us to pledge safety; bright red signs admonishing us "This is not an Exit!" and "Do not jump off the dock!" or simple statements proclaiming "Safety First;" and there is even a whiteboard chronicling the number of days we've gone without having an accident. In light of all of these warnings, and many, many more, we may "safely" conclude that our being maimed is not only possible, but very likely.

Can one imagine a more stark contrast to this than one of the Pony Express stations? There it stands, a lone, wooden building out in the middle of a vast prairie, rugged mountains rising up in the distance, an awesome expanse of deep blue canvassing the sky. Some gnarly looking guy is sitting on a porch, a long piece of grass in his mouth, eyeing a couple horses in a pen over yonder. After riding hard for seventy-five miles, a rider gallops up and decides to sit down next to the old man to enjoy the silence. The gnarly guy stares out across the landscape for a long time, and then, without turning his gaze, he suddenly asks, "Did you pledge safety today, son?"

Maybe we've grown soft over the years, a bit silky perhaps. But then again, maybe we've learned that wearing a helmet isn't such a bad idea after all, even if you do look like a dork. Either way, I believe that the same progressive spirit that resided in the heart of the Pony Express lives on in the mail delivery system of today, for we're always looking forward, ever stretching the limits of human ingenuity, always trying to move the mail faster.

Today the United States Postal Service handles 46% of the world's mail volume, with annual revenues exceeding 65 billion dollars. It's also reported that some 213 billion pieces of mail were delivered in 2006 alone. These are staggering statistics. Who could have imagined such exponential growth in the 19th century? There have even been vast improvements in cost also. It might be hard to imagine, but prices are actually more affordable now. In the early days of the Pony Express, if you wanted to mail something that weighed a ½ ounce, it would have cost you five dollars (And don't forget that five dollars went much further back then. Some estimates say that a dollar in 1860 would have been equivalent to twenty dollars now.). Later on the Pony Express would drop their rates down to a dollar per ½ ounce, but even these prices would mean spending an awful lot on your nephew's birthday card. Sorry, Tommy. Maybe next year.

All in all, the mail delivery system in America has had bold beginnings with grand advancements. But with grand advancements come great transformation, and this requires flexibility and growth. And this, in turn, requires employees to move with the tides of change, to evolve in order to accommodate new programs and new technologies. But for many of the "old timers," change is a bad word. When I first hired in, there were a number of carriers used to doing things the old way, "the right way." So when management sought to enact new and more efficient programs, along with different procedures for delivering the mail, procedures which upset long-held methods of delivery, the old schoolers stiffened their necks and protested, "No siree, Bob. Not on my watch."

Actually, at the mere mention of the word "change," most carriers begin to snort and groan like a herd of constipated rhinos. And this attitude doesn't sit well with management. Thus, in the more recent history of the Post Office, there has been a great emotional struggle between the forces of management and letter carriers as this tide of change has swept across the postal landscape. And little did I know, when I first began my career, that Bromwell, one of management's greatest warriors, a man renowned for his ability to strike fear into the hearts of the most stubborn of carriers, was going to lead a charge towards greater productivity in my office.

Chapter 8

Rise of Power

While talking with the Postmaster at the front window, a customer commented on the loud talking and laughing that could be heard in the background. The Postmaster looked in the general direction of the commotion and stated flatly, "If you go to the zoo, you expect to hear animals."

A supervisor approached a seasoned carrier nicknamed Duck and said, "Duck, you know you can't smoke in here. You'll have to put that out." The mailman slowly sucked on his cigarette, exhaled, and then said, "What will happen if I don't?" The supervisor blinked at the question. After stammering around for a moment, he said, "I don't know." With the cigarette near his lips again, Duck dryly asserted, "Well, when you find out, get back with me."

A man standing near the supervisor's desk was causing a buzz. While casing my letters, I turned to steal a glance and saw a tall, polished individual in a grey suit talking with a practiced smile. It may have been the gold watch glistening on his wrist, or his freshly polished shoes, or maybe the fifty dollar haircut that produced the overall effect, but whatever the case, this man glowed with the crisp glow of elite professionalism, a professionalism that clearly communicated, "I am a man who is used to being listened to."

I looked around at the other carriers. They too were intrigued by the figure and could be seen casting curious looks his way. I cased a couple more magazines and peered across the room again. The man was standing in the same spot, hands folded in front of him. Without moving his head, his eyes slowly scanned the room. He seemed to be pondering what was before him, contemplating the surroundings, almost as if he were solving an equation in his mind. But there was more to it than that. I could feel something else. He seemed to be measuring us. Yes. That was it. He was sizing us up.

Ah yes, management. When I first hired in as a letter carrier, I expected a number of challenges, certainly Indiana weather and dogs, but I really didn't think that my day-to-day affairs with supervision would be that terribly significant. After all, the mailman only hangs out in the office for a couple hours in the morning before he heads outside, just long enough to case up the mail and do some paper work. The boss would only be a minor part, right? Uh, no. I quickly learned just how skilled management was at making the most out of 120 minutes each morning; just how talented they are at tormenting carriers with tedious arguments regarding expected delivery times. And I soon realized that Bromwell, the man scrutinizing us on that Monday morning, was a Postmaster, nay, a managerial Sith Lord trained in the dark arts of intimidation and coercion. That's right. A Sith Lord was forever going to correct my view of management.

Helen rose from her desk and announced in a cheerful voice, "Gather around everyone. Gather around."

She walked to the center of the room, clasped her hands together and gave a spirited introduction, "As some of you may not know, we are privileged to have Kurt Bromwell in our midst. In fact, he's going to join our staff of managers for a season. He has been summoned to, uh," she paused as she searched for the right words, "assist us in our period of transition- our transition towards greater efficiency and productivity."

With her hands still clasped together, she looked over her shoulder towards Bromwell and fluttered, "Well, I imagine you have a lot you want to say in this regard." She looked towards us again, "So without further adieu, let me introduce, Mr. Kurt Bromwell."

Helen's words had certainly touched upon the real reason why Bromwell was there. From somewhere deep within the ranks of upper management, a score of number-crunching, Oh-I-love-to-stare-at-computer-spread-sheets-efficiency experts noticed that our job performance needed revival. Our current Postmaster was a mild-mannered, Indiana boy on the verge of retirement. As such, he just didn't feel the need to crack the whip nor become too involved with the demands sent down from upstairs. Instead, he was more content to sit back and let the operation run on cruise control. That was fine by us, but our good friends, the efficiency experts, had other ideas. They wanted to see some improvements and pronto. And so they summoned Bromwell for this special task.

Helen scurried out of the way while Bromwell confidently strode to the center of the room. He grabbed a chair and lifted one leg onto it, leaned casually and exuded confidence. Polished words then began to flow effortlessly from his mouth. His voice was clear and arresting, though, according to his volume, one might have supposed he were speaking to a crowd ten times our size. And one could scarcely miss the harmonious interplay between his gestures and words. Resolute declarations were attended with a pumping fist. Calls for us to rise to the challenge were accompanied by inviting palms. One hand found a pocket when he began to speak about team spirit and greater productivity. And words such as "cooperation," "new objectives" and "smooth transition" were wed together seamlessly as he moved through the bulk of his speech. He wrapped his talk up with a quote from Abraham Lincoln and then stood tall and proud amid a band of bewildered mailmen.

A smile formed on his face. It was like a parking lot full of white Corvettes.

The union stewards were all but cracking their knuckles by the end. Others merely blinked, clearly in shock. I sensed something was amiss, but held my suspicions in check. In light of the fact that I was still very new to the Post Office and didn't have a firm grasp on the ins and outs of postal life, any definitive judgments about the man seemed brash. Besides, there were elements to his speech that rang true, at least a little bit. As he spoke about our need to "tighten things up," (meaning of course a mailman's tendency to hang out at a tavern too long or chat with patrons too much) I considered some of the carriers around me. Duck could be seen leaning up against his case with a lazy expression etched across his face. This was the guy caught by management taking twenty-one minutes to drop off the mail inside an Eagles lodge. When he finally came out, management drove up and asked him if he knew how long he was in there. He shrugged.

"Twenty-one minutes!" They informed him, "That's how long you were in there."

Duck shot them a relieved expression, "Twenty-one minutes? Shwooo. It's a good thing you weren't around yesterday."

There was also Big Daddy, an older mailman with a long, grey pony tail dangling down his back. He and I often ate lunch together, and as our thirty-minute lunch break neared its end, I would stand up and get rebuked, "Brownie, what are you doing? Sit down. We just got here." For many of the carriers, the thirty-minute allotment for lunch was a negotiable figure, a good starting point, if you will.

Oh, and I can't fail to mention "Two Guys" either, a man of immense girth, weighing easily three hundred pounds, a giant of sorts who was either heading towards the bathroom, in the bathroom or leaving the bathroom. I suppose if I drank a two liter of Mountain Dew each morning, I'd be hanging out in the bathroom a lot also. But it wasn't simply his frequent bathroom breaks that perturbed management so much. He could often be heard bellowing with laughter while in there. And if one were to venture in to see what all the excitement was about, they would see him standing in front of the mirror, wiping his glasses for about the three hundredth time, discussing, with fantastic jocularity, the latest Seinfeld episode with the guy in stall three.

So, in all fairness, there were some rough edges here and there. I suppose Bromwell had a right to be concerned about such matters. True enough. But on the other hand, most of these guys had put in many, many years of hard work for the Post Office and were slowing down a bit. It was only natural. So anyway, I could see things both ways. With a little understanding and good leadership, Bromwell could probably achieve his objectives without ruffling too many feathers. Maybe we could work as a team after all, and maybe we could attain some measure of harmony. With a little respect and a dash of thoughtfulness, we could surely achieve our goals together.

Chapter 9

A Rude Awakening

Determine that the thing can and shall be done, and then we shall find the way.

-Abraham Lincoln-

A knot formed in my stomach on the 23rd ring.

"Honey, why don't you just go ahead and answer the phone?" my wife mumbled, pulling the blankets up over her head.

The phone continued to ring.

I moaned at the prospect of answering the call. It was no doubt Helen wanting me to come in on my day off. But I wasn't about to answer the phone. While firmly fixed to my bed, I had every intention of doing absolutely nothing on that dreary Monday morning. And so long as I avoided contact with management, they couldn't tell me to come in to work.

That's how things operate at the Post Office. When there's a NS posted next to your name on the schedule (NS means "Not Scheduled"), it's written lightly and with a pencil. If somebody calls in sick, or if management simply changes their mind and wants to move a lot of mail that day, they can, and usually will, give you an early morning wake-up call. But here's the thing. A carrier has absolutely no obligation to go into work, so long as they don't hear a command from the lips of management to do so. It's as simple as that. Just ignore the incessant ringing and the day is all yours. But that's kind of difficult when it's 5:43 AM.

"Tell me why we don't have an answering machine?" I asked, not expecting an answer.

My wife muttered something about going to Wal-Mart.

After the 33rd ring, there followed silence.

Even though the ringing had stopped, I still had an uneasy feeling in the pit of my stomach. I could imagine Helen sitting in her swivel chair, fingers tapping the desk, face marked with annoyance.

She has to know I'm home. Where else would I be at a quarter till six? What if a couple people called in sick today? Maybe they really do need me... No, it doesn't matter. It's my day off. It's my right to stay home... But what about tomorrow? What will I do when I see her? Shrug my shoulders and offer up a goofy smile? Ignore her? Act like everything's fine. She'll know that I heard the phone. She'll see right through me. What if they really need me...?

When these thoughts began to creep into my mind, I was really close to giving in. But I reached deep down inside of myself and regained control. Days off for new carriers are a rarity, and I really wanted a break. So once I was sure that my apprehensions had been successfully bound and locked up, I buried my face in my pillow and summoned sleep afresh.

About fifteen minutes later, the phone started to ring again.

"I know, I know," I said to my wife, "But I really don't want to go in today. Yes, I'm sure I won't get in trouble. No, she'll give up soon. Don't worry."

After about thirty rings, the phone went silent.

I stared at the ceiling, while the minutes rolled by. By this point, I had pretty much given up on trying to sleep and resigned myself to laying around until I couldn't resist getting up for a bowl of cereal.

Suddenly there was the sound of "Bam! Bam! Bam!" on my front door.

My wife and I bolted upright in bed. "Bam! Bam! Bam!" went the sound again, this time even louder.

I looked over at my wife with an expression like, "You don't think..."

I hopped out of bed and started for the front door. If I hadn't been so overwhelmed with astonishment, I might have noticed the pounding heart in my chest.

When I entered the living room and could see the front door, the hard knocking started up again. The house literally shook as each tremendous hit pounded against the door in rapid succession. This was no mere knock anymore. Someone was obviously hitting the door with an open hand. And hard.

When I neared the door, maybe about four or five paces away, I looked down in amazement as the little gold handle began to jiggle and forcibly shake. I couldn't believe my eyes. Whoever was beating on my door was apparently also trying to get in!

When the handle calmed down, I cautiously unlocked it. A swinging door revealed a man standing on my front step, his face contorted with a scowl. It was Bromwell.

As the early morning sunlight cast its first rays across the neighborhood, my features were illuminated by the soft glow of dawn. And so Bromwell would have seen a glowing young man standing in a doorway, mouth gaping, hair wild, outfitted with uneven tube socks and a crumpled T-shirt hanging loosely over a pair of boxers.

Unfazed by my appearance, he immediately ushered forth a command, "You're coming to work today. Be there in thirty minutes."

As I stood there watching Bromwell with his arms folded tightly over a power suit that was fully living up to its name, his stern gaze fixed on me, I found myself unable to form even one coherent syllable. As my mouth twitched, searching for something to say, Bromwell moved forward with a finger aimed at my heart, "I will see you in 30 minutes." With that, he spun around and promptly left.

I shut the door slowly, trying to comprehend what had just transpired. *Did that really just happen?* I thought to myself. *Can they actually come to your house and drag you out of bed?*

By now my wife was standing in the doorway to our bedroom. "Who was that?" She asked.

My thoughts were racing, but I managed to say, "That was Bromwell." I paused. "The Postmaster."

It didn't take long for the news of what had happened to circulate around the Post Office. While standing in the bathroom, I recounted my story to "Two Guys" and a few other intrigued carriers, making sure not to leave out any juicy details. Once that initial deposit was planted in their ears, they inevitably shared the newly acquired information with the people casing next to them.

From there, it's only a matter of time before a clerk picks up the story and broadcasts it amongst their kind. And when they know, everyone knows. For it should be noted that postal clerks resemble something like an information highway. They're our Google search engine. If we want to know something about the daily affairs of management, or the latest intrigue surrounding someone's hair color choice, or possibly a developing tale of sordid love, well, then we need only to tap into their knowledge data base and download the desired information. But there's a drawback. Once the information goes public, management often catches wind of the latest and tastiest happenings. It therefore didn't take long before Helen became aware of the buzz surrounding the Bromwell incident and warned him that the story was gaining popularity. Being a crafty man, he thought it would be prudent to proactively deal with the problem by summoning me to his chambers for a personal meeting.

Helen walked up to my case and said, "The Postmaster would like to have a word with you." The union steward was with her. I didn't know it at the time, but when you have a meeting with management that also involves the union steward, it typically means something serious is going to be discussed. Both sides want a witness present, so as to keep the facts straight.

I set down my letters and followed Helen to the Postmaster's office. As we wove our way through a snaking hallway, I shot a concerned look toward the union steward as he leaned in close and whispered, "You don't have to say anything, and I don't recommend that you do. Leave the talking up to me. Okay?"

I nodded and wiped my suddenly clammy hands on my pants.

When we entered Bromwell's office, he was sitting behind a large, cherry desk with his arms resting easily on the smooth surface. Sunlight poured in through a picture window in the rear, illuminating his austere features.

His hand motioned for us to sit down in two cushioned chairs before him. Helen positioned herself to his left and regarded us coolly. With his elbows on the desk, arms forming a pyramid, fingers loosely laced together, Bromwell initiated the discussion,

"It's been reported that you think there has been a problem with certain events of late." He paused to see if I would say anything.

I didn't.

He looked down at his desk, then back up, "I want you to know that if you think there is a problem, a problem of any sort, then I share your concerns. I am committed to the well being of my employees and want you to know that you should feel free to contact someone about any issues that might be troubling you."

With that, Bromwell picked up a small business card and handed it to me. It was something like an I-CARE hotline, a phone number designed for mailmen struggling with psychological problems, or who simply need to talk about personal issues.

When I looked up from the card, Bromwell was leaning back in his chair, legs crossed, a smug expression rimmed with sunlight. As he rocked back and forth slowly, I realized that there was nothing I could do. He had won this encounter. But I learned something that day. I learned that management is a sly lot, a cunning team of individuals that can't be trusted no matter how white their smiles might be.

Yes, it was on that day that I, Austin Brown, a still very green mailman, decided he would play his cards differently from that day forward. He would learn from his mistakes and adjust accordingly. He wouldn't be outdone by Bromwell again. Next time, he would be ready.

Chapter 10

A Young Jedi Fights Back

"Stopped they must be; on this all depends. Only a fully-trained Jedi Knight, with the Force as his ally, will conquer Vader and his Emperor."

-Yoda-

I felt more than a little smug, as my newly acquired answering machine prompted Helen to leave yet another message.

"After the beep, Helen," I said self amusingly along with the machine, "and I'll get right back with ya."

She didn't leave a message.

A moment later, I rolled out of bed and headed off to the kitchen. A blinking red four on my answering machine beckoned me. I pressed play.

(Synthesized voice) You have four new messages.
Message one, 6:11AM.
"Good morning, Austin. It's Helen. I need you to come in today. We had a sick call. (Pause) Ok, give me a call. Thanks."

Message two, 6:18AM.
"Austin, you there? Austin? (Longish pause) We had a sick call. I really need you to pick up. (Voice cranked a little higher) Austin, wake up! We really need you here, ok? Call me as soon as you get this. Right away. Helen."

Message three, 6:22AM.
(Perturbed, panicky and impatient) "Austin? Austin, you there? Pick up..." (Long pause followed by an audible sigh) Click.

Message four, 6:29AM.

Only the rattling sound of a phone returning to its cradle.

While standing there, leaning against the fridge, grinning from east to west, I listened to all four messages. Of course, I had already heard each one while lying in bed, but I couldn't resist giving them another go. The third one especially made me chuckle.

I glanced at the clock on the microwave. 6:54AM.

She's finally given up, I thought to myself. And so I celebrated by making myself a bowl of Cheerios.

While sniffing the milk, I silently praised my new answering machine.

That's all they can do. Just leave a message, because, yes, that's right, I'm not available right now. I'll be the one to get back with you.

I continued to smile.

I love my answering machine.

It was the first time my answering machine had been given a chance to show off its usefulness since my initial encounter with Bromwell. In the four or so weeks following that dreadful morning, management worked me every day. So I hadn't yet been given an opportunity to test out the new equipment. But on this glorious Wednesday, the schedule did in fact have a "NS" by my name. And even though I didn't have anything special to do except maybe watch Regis and Kathie Lee while painting some fantasy miniatures, I wasn't about to answer the phone. Not even if every last carrier in Indiana called in sick. Not even if the fate of the world depended on my answering the phone. I wanted the day off. No. More than that. Like those explorers of old who, upon finding some new luscious land, stab a waving flag into the ground, I claimed this day as my own and would defend it to the bitter end. And my new answering machine would provide me with the necessary means of protection. It would be my shield. My guardian. My anti-Bromwell buffer. *Yes, just leave a message and I'll be the one to get back with you.*

All the power was in my court. Or so I thought.

I plopped down on the couch and flipped on the TV.

The Cheerios were outstanding and brought immeasurable delight, and for several minutes, I didn't hear anything but the musical sound of crunching.

That's when the thought occurred to me.

I'm not sure why it didn't dawn on me before, but for whatever reason, it escaped my notice. Only while shoveling another spoonful of cereal into my mouth did I think to question the assumption that all the power was in fact in my court.

Now what's stopping Bromwell from coming out again? My answering machine? But why would that stop him? Well, Austin, because they left a message, and they're waiting for you to call them back. But what if they don't wait, moron? What if he decides to pay you another visit? Give you a little wakeup call of his own?

My spoon hovered in a fixed state somewhere between the bowl and my mouth.

I glanced out the living room window. There in the driveway sat my red 1991 Ford Tempo, the car I always drove to work.

He'll know I'm here. No, maybe not. Think clearly, Austin. You have two cars. I could be out in the other one. But wait. Does he know we have two cars? Why would he know? He'd have to figure I have two cars, right?

My living room window, with its curtains pulled back, suddenly seemed to take on gigantic proportions, as though the whole side of my house were one gaping hole, with me sitting there, in full display, like an insect in a jar.

I quickly pulled the curtains and returned to the couch and scooped up a spoonful of now soggy Cheerios.

That's when I heard the sound of tires on pavement.

I bolted upright and dared a look. Through the soft and somewhat opaque curtains, white and sheer by the design of my wife, I could just barely make out the outline of a car. With my cereal bowl in one hand, and the remote in the other, I cautiously crept closer for a better look.

Bromwell!

At the sight of the driver's door swinging open and one foot planting itself on the ground, a seismic shot of adrenaline shot through my system, causing the world to spin and the colors to flare.

It's Bromwell!

I instantly dropped to the ground and began crawling commando style away from the window. At that moment, all sense left me. I just crawled as fast as I could, spilling milk everywhere while wiggling madly, trying desperately to make it to the bedroom.

This is ridiculous, I thought to myself pausing briefly in the doorway of my bedroom. *Get a grip, Austin!* But when I heard not one, but two car doors slam shut, a fresh wave of terror shot through me. The strength of the feeling was astonishing. I felt the urge to bolt, to make a mad dash for the backdoor, or a window, to simply run off into the woods like an convict catching the distant sound of barking dogs.

I'm not proud of this fact, but I actually hid in my bedroom closet.

The first round of knocks sounded on the front door. They were hard, but not shake the house hard. I stood motionless in my closet trying to think what to do.

Did he see me drop to the ground? Did he catch sight of my legs while I was crawling away? What if he did? What if he knows I'm in here?

More knocking.

What if he knows!

There was a part of me that wanted to turn myself in, to just give up and go on in to work. *Is it really worth all this to stay home?* But I gathered myself. I reminded myself that Bromwell couldn't win. He couldn't have the pleasure of capturing me again. If I cowered before him now, I would forever be conquered and enslaved to do his bidding. That last thought gave me resolve.

A nearby window would permit a glimpse of the front steps, if I pressed my face up against the glass and peered out at a sharp angle. The temptation was irresistible. I had to chance a look. So moving with all the stealth of a black cat, I crept over to the window and cautiously peeked out.

If one of the busybodies in our neighborhood, perhaps Mrs. Shelby, a particularly snoopy neighbor across the street, happened to be watching the unfolding scene out her window, she would have seen two well-dressed men on my front steps. As one of the two men continued to knock on the door, she would have seen the other looking around the area, hands in pocket, with a hint of discomfort on his face. About twenty feet from their location, peering out through a thin partition of a curtain, she might have also detected a single spying eye, an eye that suddenly widened, as if in shock, as it locked onto the figure standing beside Bromwell.

He brought Stewart with him!

Stewart was a supervisor in training; a thirty-something who looked remarkably like Magnum P.I. He even sported a large pair of dark sunglasses and had an affinity for tight shorts.

I was surprised to see him here. He was one of the few managers who knew how to get along with the carriers, and I had taken an early liking to him. But I supposed that he had little choice in the matter. If Bromwell wanted him by his side, he would be by his side.

"Bromwell must want a witness this time," I muttered under my breath.

But he didn't need a witness with this kind of behavior; for although the knocks continued unabated, they weren't threatening. And I didn't see his hand go anywhere near the handle. That, of course, wouldn't be something he'd want witnessed.

I slowly slid away from the curtains and retreated back to the closet. After what seemed like an eternity, the knocking finally stopped. Then I heard their car start up. Then I heard them drive away. And then there was a profound silence.

By infinite and cautious degrees, I slowly emerged from the bedroom.

✓ Small victory for the mailman.

So the answering machine didn't quite work out as expected. Not only did it fail to ward off Bromwell's managerial house call, but it made for an extremely awkward meeting with Helen the next day. I dreaded seeing her, knowing that she would probably confront me. And sure enough, just as I suspected, right after clocking in, she wasted no time in making a bee line for me, lips pursed, face set like flint.

"Did you get my messages?" She asked, arms folded defensively before her.

"Um, yes," I answered slowly, creating more space between us.

"Why didn't you call me back?"

Sweat formed on my brow.

"Well, uh, if a person isn't around. Well, suppose someone is gone. Gone all day. Do you want them to call back later, even if it's like, say, midnight?"

Her eyes narrowed. "We'd like to hear from you as soon as possible."

"Oh, ok."

"So were you gone?"

I coughed, "Excuse me?"

"Yesterday. Were you there?"

"I did some running around."

Well, listen," She began with an ill-pleased look, "We need to be able to reach you. Understand?"

"Mhm."

"Be sure to answer your phone next time."

I stood motionless.

"Will you do that?"

I hesitated. She didn't blink.

My response followed, "Uhuh."

Believe it or not, that ended up being true. A few weeks later during the early morning hours of a scheduled day off, the phone rang, and I immediately bolted out of bed and ran towards the front door, shouting back to my wife, "When I'm gone, answer the phone."

My puzzled wife exclaimed, "What! Me?"

"Just tell her I'm out."

"*What?!?*"

I jumped in the car and drove off.

My wife reluctantly answered the phone.

"Hello."

"Oh, hi. Can I speak with Austin, please?"

"Um, he's out."

(Confused pause)

"Ok... Do you know when he'll be back?"

"Not really."

"You don't know when he'll be back?"

"I'm sorry. I don't."

(Another long pause)

"I see. Well, when you do see him, tell him Helen called and that she'd like to hear from him."

"I will do that."

That wasn't my greatest moment of chivalry, and so feeling bad about putting my wife in that position, I vowed never to do it again. Not that I had much of a choice in the matter.

And so in the days to come, the cat and mouse game continued, with new evasive measures being continually adopted. Parking my car elsewhere proved most fruitful. They wouldn't knock nearly as long that way. And with each new encounter, I grew more and more comfortable, eventually becoming so comfortable with the situation that I could sit in the corner of my house and eat my cereal before it grew soggy.

For the life of her, my wife could never understand why I would go to such lengths.

"Is it really worth it?" She would ask. "I mean, is it worth this much trouble?"

Totally.

It was never intended for Bromwell to remain Postmaster at our office for very long. So when he finally left to terrorize another crew of unsuspecting carriers elsewhere, great rejoicing erupted from our ranks. Stories about the man were soon swapped and told with a new found mirth. Nervous ticks began to melt away. And there was even a sharp decline in the use of profanity. I became something of a celebrity too. This was due not only to his having frequented my house on several occasions, but due also in part to his having sent the janitor and the maintenance man out to my home in an attempt to trick me into answering the door. So even to this day there are those who will bang on something hollow, mimicking the sound of hard knocking, shouting, "Brownie! I know you're in there. Come out!" At other times, when the phone can be heard ringing loudly throughout the workroom floor, someone will cry out, "Don't answer it, Austin. Just run! Run!"

Unfortunately our days of jubilation were short-lived, for as is so often the case in our world, one tyrant is merely replaced by another. And so in Bromwell's stead there has arisen a long chain of successive managers who, with studious imitation and careful study, have perpetuated the ideals of the Postmaster's insidious legacy. The years since that time have therefore been filled with many of the same Bromwellian tactics, cunning devices and silly squabbles that we carriers have come to enjoy like a persistent toothache. "Two Guys" is particularly fond of the word "Shawshank" as a description of our office since the days of Bromwell. And sometimes, while whispering in the ear of some new employee, he can be heard mixing his metaphors, "Welcome to Shawshank. Watch out for the Gestapo."

The frustrations that exist between management and letter carriers can ultimately be boiled down to one primary issue.

Time.

Time is everything at the Post Office, because time is money. And if you don't make money, then some other business will come along and show you how it's done. Thus, managers are pressured to produce better numbers and reduce overtime, figure out ways to get more mail out, and faster. But oftentimes, carriers understand phrases like "greater efficiency" and "more productivity" as merely code words for "run until your knees explode" or "skip your lunch and take a bunch." This results in a collision of wills and an almost daily struggle over delivery times.

Now in order to understand what it means to bicker over delivery times, one needs to understand that mail volumes fluxuate each and every day. Sometimes mail volumes are light. But at other times there are enormous piles of the stuff- heaping piles of parcels, stacks of fliers, horrendously heavy department store catalogs, product samples- and if you were to actually case it all up and deliver it all in one day, you'd first need a shot of morphine and then, much later, a miner's helmet with fresh batteries.

In order to deal with heavy volumes, we curtail some of the bulk rate mail over a two or three-day period. In other words, a portion of the mail is held back and taken out more gradually. This is where debate enters the picture, because we need to come to an agreement with management over how much mail is going to be moved as well as how long it's going to take for us to deliver it.

At some point in the morning, the supervisor yells out, "thirty-nine ninety-six." This is the number of a form that carriers fill out in order to provide management with an estimate of how long it's going to take them to deliver all the mail that day. If you think it's going to take nine hours, then you write nine hours. If you think it's going to take infinity, then you write, "Ha, ha, ha." There's also a small box for explaining why it's going to take as long as you suppose it will. Those who are in a particularly chipper mood use this space to draw pictures of mailmen experiencing heat stroke or possibly stick men carrying bags filled with humongous parcels, certified letters and other such items that add extra time to one's day. After filling out the form, you take it up to the supervisor's desk and return to casing the mail. If perchance you actually wrote a number that they deem acceptable, then you won't hear from them and you're free to go about your work. If there's a discrepancy between your figure and theirs, which is often the case, then you can expect to receive a visit from a sour-faced supervisor.

Here's what happens. The manager, let's call him Phil, strolls over with a clipboard and ponders the mail stacked up around your case. As his eyes move from the clipboard to the mail and then back to the clipboard, his expression is like that of a man contemplating the taste of some new cuisine. As his head bobs ever so slightly, and as his tongue works in secret, his eyes move with each quiet thought. And then, as if a verdict about the taste has been reached, he looks up and says, "The computer has you about four minutes over, if you take it all."

By "four minutes over," he's referring to those four minutes that extend past the eighth working hour, which is overtime for us. By "computer" he's referring not so much to the little white machine sitting on his desk, but to a program that provides him with an estimation of how long it should take us to deliver the mail that day. This is supposedly based upon an average of our previous delivery times, but because we haven't yet sprouted wings, the estimates are more than a little suspicious to us. With differing degrees of exasperation, we reply, "Four minutes over?!? You're kidding, right?" This effectively warms up the discussion.

Depending on the supervisors own peculiar disposition, a carrier can usually expect one of several, though sometimes nuanced, responses. The first is intimidation. After a fruitless back and forth exchange, the manager gets right in your face and says, "You will take X amount of mail and you will get back in eight hours." This kind of behavior is similar to that of the warrior on the battlefield who can be heard roaring terrible threats, while waving his broadsword high in the air. Just as the warrior's opponent will often flee at the sight of such ominous strength, so too newer mailmen often buckle under the pressure and yield to the supervisor's will. Some of the more seasoned carriers, however, are tempted to unbuckle their own battle axes and rush headlong into battle, but they know it's far more effective to raise the shield of safety and exclaim, "Sir, I'm concerned that if I take this much mail and try to get back in eight hours, I will be forced to engage in unsafe walking or driving habits. Safety first, right?"

Sometimes management looks hurt or wounded, almost as if you said something bad about their nose or their weight. With eyes full of pain, mouth open, and possibly sighing, their entire countenance says, "I really thought you were better than this." Those who have tender consciousness are especially prone to fall for this one. And it can sometimes take quite a while before these carriers realize that the emotional display is nothing more than a ruse. For when they're out running down the street, misdelivering mail left and right or hitting mail boxes with their truck, they soon learn that management conveniently forgets that it was they who encouraged the reckless abandon. And as management pulls the disciplinary lever, dropping the tender-hearted carrier down to their postal demise, they will notice that the look of disappointment, the look that so frequently decorated their supervisor's face, is suddenly strangely absent.

Female carriers have the advantage of being able to summon tears as a counter to such managerial tactics. Men, however, are far more likely to start cussing before they can reach the place where crying can be achieved, and so they have to acquire an especially thick skin that's capable of withstanding even the most tortured of expressions. This is made more difficult when management changes tactics by casting shadows of doubt upon one's integrity. They accomplish this, not so much by stating the point bluntly, but by utilizing subtlety. "Efficient carriers could do it," they say. Or, "Should I be made aware of some problem that is affecting your job performance?" "Have you been feeling unwell lately? "Things all right at home?"

The place where mailmen explore these matters in far more delicious detail is our monthly union meetings. Gathering around a large table down at the local VFW, carriers moan and wail for hours on end as the union president unpacks the latest, gory developments in postal life. The mood usually lightens once beer and pizza are served, but even then there are moments when the laughing is interrupted when someone recounts a grievous encounter with management. If things become too lively, whether from too much joking or angry interjection, the president promptly bangs his wooden hammer on a small anvil, "Quiet down, everyone. Quiet down. I said, 'Quiet down!' Listen, section 209.4 tells us that- Hey, Keith, can you hand me a napkin, thanks- official protocol tells us that if we can't fit all our parcels into the cart, then we are allowed to..." And thus the discussion continues unabated for quite a very long time.

"Two Guys," after having consumed a barrel or two of alcohol, becomes loud and interruptive, often showering people with gummy chunks of pizza as he rambles on about his own frustrations with management. Those sitting next to the giant scoot away, while others, almost as if they were watching someone toss knives at an apple atop another's head, cringe and groan as meaty projectiles arc across the table dangerously close to open drinks. By this point in the evening, the president recognizes that things are moving swiftly beyond recovery, so he recaps a few of the more pertinent points and then announces that the meeting is officially adjourned. Most of the carriers go home, but there are always those who choose to remain behind and drink until somebody like Bromwell doesn't seem quite so bad.

The young Jedi hoping to understand more fully the psychological stratagems of management should attend these meetings for a more thorough and systematic breakdown of what might not be discerned through personal experience alone. Much to the dismay of my fellow employees, I typically refrain from attending these monthly meetings, choosing instead to catch up while milling around the time clock the next morning. I can usually count on others to rehash important news or share juicy stories, but if not, then there is always lunch. That is the next best place for exploring the strategies of management.

For the most part, my days with Bromwell were sufficient training grounds. Having come out of that trial still possessing my sanity, as well as a few previously undiscovered tactics in managerial avoidance, I have been awarded the status, Jedi Knight.

Chapter 11

The *Rippus Leggus Offitus*

"The shepherd's dog barked fiercely when one of these alien-looking
men appeared on the upland, dark against the early winter sunset;
for what dog likes a figure bent under a heavy bag?"

-George Eliot, *Silas Marner*-

———————————

Dogs are everywhere.

According to the National Humane Society, there are
approximately sixty-five million of the things running around the
United States. That's a disturbing statistic, for it means that
mailmen are outnumbered 295 to 1. Even King Leonidas didn't
face those kinds of odds. And given the fact that the population of
America runs around 300 million, simple division says that there
are 4.6 people for every one dog.

So like I said. Dogs are everywhere.

And what this means for the mailman is that sooner or later
(usually sooner), he's going to have an unpleasant confrontation
with a dog. It's kind of like getting pooped on by a bird or stung by
a bee. I can expect both to happen about once each year while
walking the mail.

Unfortunately, dog attacks happen more frequently than
that, but most don't register too high on the heinosity meter. I'd
say that about one or two encounters each year breaks an eight on
the doggy Richter scale.

That's not too bad, I guess. But it's not real good either.

The USPS expects about 2,800 carriers to be bitten
annually. This figure, of course, only reflects those who actually get
munched on. There are countless others who come out unscathed
and don't make the record books.

Personally, I've lost count of how many times I've been attacked. It's a lot though. But I haven't lost count of how many times I've been attacked by a pit bull.

It's three.

No one forgets that.

And that's three too many times, because pit bulls are the big daddies of Doggydom. The grand generals of the furry army. The truly feared, and the truly deadly.

Now in some cities, like Denver, New York City and Chicago, pit bulls have been outright banned. But scroll down a list of dog bans in Indiana and it soon becomes apparent that Hoosiers aren't ready to give up their terrible terriers. But I really didn't need a website to tell me that. They're common enough in my neck of the woods. People love them. Adore them. Some own two or three.

It isn't just rednecks who own them either. That's what I used to think. But there are all kinds. In fact, Mark Twain owned one. So did Thomas Edison. Even Helen Keller. It was named Stubby. Add to the list, Michael J Fox, President Woodrow Wilson, Mary Tyler Moore, Jon Stewart and TV cook, Rachael Ray.

If given the chance, I'm not sure I'd outright ban the dogs from my state. No need for that kind of regulation. If people want to own a pit bull, fine. Own a pit bull. But if the dog attacks a non-intruder, I can't say that I wouldn't be opposed to sentencing the owner to six months of hard labor at a camp in Siberia. That seems about right to me.

Of course, there are plenty of people who claim that pit bulls are entirely safe and wouldn't so much as hurt a fly. Some argue they're misunderstood and caricatured as evil because of the actions of a demented few. "A lot of myths," they say, "There are a lot of myths surrounding the pit bull."

Well, maybe.

In my reading on the breed, I naturally checked out Wikipedia[1]. And it just so happened that there was a section

---

[1] It should be borne in mind that Wikipedia is an ever evolving manuscript. The following quotations were present in the year 2007. In May of 2008, the article added: "Editors are currently in dispute concerning points of view expressed in

entitled "Urban Myths." In it, the contributors sought to dispel legendary or fictitious notions surrounding the pit bull.

Allow me to share a few of the findings. They are illuminating.

Myth: Pit bulls don't feel pain.

Fact: Pit bulls have the same nervous system of any other breed, and they can and do feel pain. Historically, those dogs that would tolerate or ignore discomfort and pain and finish the task they were required to perform were the dogs so bred, and the sort dog breeders strove to produce. This is the trait of "gameness" that so many breed fanciers speak of, which may be defined as, "The desire to continue on and/or complete a task despite pain and discomfort." Therefore, the difficulty in deterring a pit bull from its task is in fact not an inability to feel pain but rather a desirable trait in any trained working dog.

Well, I feel so much better now. Don't you? It's good to know that while you're hitting the pit bull in the face with a club, it does in fact feel some discomfort.

Myth: Pit bulls are unique in that they are the only dogs not affected by capsaicin-based dog-repellent spray.

Fact: Many other dog breeds also display this resistance to pepper spray when they are attacking. Documented cases include bull mastiffs, Rottweilers and many German shepherds (including Police K9s).

Isn't that dandy? They don't deny that the pit bulls have a natural resistance to pepper spray, but only that he isn't entirely unique in this respect.

I can vouch for this. On one occasion, I ran into a slightly overweight, wrinkly faced dog (something that looked like a mastiff, although I'm not sure), that decided he didn't like me hanging

---

this. Please help to discuss and resolve the dispute before removing this message." Ah, very good. Allow me to shed light on the matter then.

around his neighborhood. When the dog came in to dine, I gave him a drink of orange Kool-Aid. The pepper spray hit him right in the mouth, and to my utter surprise, he simply opened wider and wiggled his tongue around in a kind of, "Not too bad really. A bit spicy, but pretty good on the whole." I must have emptied half a can of mace on him, but never once did he seem to be in any kind of serious pain. The spraying annoyed him, like how a child might complain about another kid splashing in a pool too much, but that was about it.

Myth: Pit bulls are the only dogs that can keep attacking after being severely wounded.

Fact: It is also untrue that the pit bull is the only dog that will keep attacking after being sub-lethally shot. Rottweilers, mastiffs and German shepherds have all exhibited this capacity.

Well, there you have it. It ends up that the pit bull isn't the only Terminator out there. He, along with some of his other buddies, can keep crawling after Sarah Connor even after having been shot by an entire police squad.

It's good to know the truth about such "urban legends," isn't it?

After my first encounter with a pit bull, the incident recounted back in chapter one, I'm proud to say that I didn't wet my pants. I did tremble, however. And I couldn't draw one of those really deep cleansing breaths. Every atom in my body was tingling. And so I just sat in my truck and blinked, for a very long time.

As for the old man in the Buick, he left without a word and to this very day I still don't know who he is. I wish I did. I'd fall down and kiss the man's hands with deep affection. I'd pour my gratitude with tambourine and sweet melody, singing,

"Oh, victory is yours, old man, so true,
With Buick power you ran the dog through.

With courage from on high you vanquished the foe,
With unwavering bravery you dispelled Kujo.

The dog's teeth flared, his eyes shot fire,
But with one great "rev" you spun your tire.
No gun, no bullet can hurt the Pit Bull,
But with bumper and skill you aimed for his skull.

Now I am free, my limbs intact,
So listen all, for this is a fact;
My knight who rides in grey, dull steel,
Dost triumph proud behind the wheel."

I really do wish that I could thank the old man for all he did, but he chose to ride off into the sunset like a true hero. I like to imagine him pausing briefly on the horizon, a black silhouette against the dipping sun, waving his low brimmed hat high in the air. May your days be long and sweet my old friend. Ride on man. Ride on.

The whole dog attack thing is bizarre. One second we're walking along and everything is fine, and the next, some grisly dog is snacking on us. And after having beaten the thing off, we're supposed to keep walking in a normal and easy fashion as if something hadn't just tried to devour us. It's not possible, because after an attack, our legs feel so weak, so completely filled with Jell-O, that we can't, no matter how hard we try, no matter how much we want to save face before the neighborhood- who certainly are looking out their windows in wonder because of all the cussing they just heard- walk casually.

Thankfully, the staggering usually wears off after twenty minutes.

But what can sometimes last for hours, even days, is an acute hypersensitivity to sound. Seriously. Every single sound is amplified a hundredfold, and you feel as jumpy as an alley cat in a foreign neighborhood.

A twig snaps four blocks away. You hear it.

An insect falls off a tree branch. You hear it.

Someone shuts a car door. You jump six feet in the air.

I've literally spun around, spray in hand, body coiled like a tight spring, only to see a leaf tumbling across the ground a few feet away. It sounded just like a sprinting dog. Of course, each time I execute this startled, spinning maneuver, random onlookers squint and stare at the strange behavior; and so, often, to avoid looking like a complete loon, I try to smooth out the motion by performing a number of stretching exercises, as if that were my intention all along, or I drop down to tie my shoes, "Never mind the Kung Fu stance, bewildered patrons. Just a mailman trying his shoes. Carry on. Carry on."

I can't imagine how jumpy one must be after having been mauled by a pit bull. Unfortunately, letter carrier Bryon Jenkins knows. One day, while making his normal rounds along the sidewalks of sunny California, he paused briefly before the fence-lined home of "Chucky," a massive pit bull, who, on this particular day, was lying comfortably in the front yard. Feeling uneasy, Bryon decided to skip the house. But just before he reached the next stop, the dog leapt over the four-foot-tall fence and pinned him to the ground, viciously biting both his face and neck. Recalling the incident, Bryon said he couldn't remember anything except waking up and seeing paramedics working frantically over him. Fortunately, some people nearby called 911 and came to his immediate aid. Doctors had to reattach Bryon's bottom lip, which was ripped off, and perform reconstructive surgery on his face.

A female carrier near Chicago, who experienced a similar kind of attack, requiring countless stitches for her injuries, expressed her own hesitations this way, "I'm a little nervous about going back to work," she said. "Kind of scared."

Yeah, to say the least.

So why in the world does the dog so hate the mailman? What's their beef?

People ask me this all the time. They look at their dog's behavior, or the behavior of other dogs, and scratch their heads in wonder. "What is it," they marvel, "that drives the dog to such blind hatred?"

Here some pick up their wild dogs and repeat over and over again, "Now, Muffin. Oh, Muh-fiiiiiiiin. Ha-ha, Muffin it's only the mailman. He doesn't want to hurt you, Muffin, honey..." And as the dog desperately tries to free itself, they continue to chant the Muffin mantra, all the while gazing affectionately at their furry terrorist.

As far as rational patrons are concerned, I've heard all kinds of theories as to why dogs go nuts when the mailman comes around.

Some say, "It's that uniform of yours. That blue shirt is like waving a red flag in front of a bull." There is much to commend this explanation, for there have been times when I have returned home from work, and upon coming into plain view of the neighbor's dog, which under normal circumstances wouldn't give me a second glance, he instantly hops up and starts barking. Why? Why else would he bark at me if weren't for my uniform? But alas, dogs appear to dislike nearly all uniforms. They snarl at the UPS man, yap at the meter man and have a hay day with those paired-up Mormon boys. No, we're going to have to say that this answer, if taken alone, cannot account for the particular hatred the dog has for the mailman.

Another theory centers on the mailman's bag. "Get rid of that bag of yours," they say, "and they'll all turn into sweet pups." But when a mailman drops off a parcel at a house, thus leaving his bag in his truck, the dog carries on with the same intensity and fervor. Thus, a careful analysis of bag to no-bag situations yields zero evidence that the satchel evokes more passion from the dog.

Some point to fear? Does the dog engage in its theatrics simply because he smells fear? This one is easily disproved. For I can assure you that most mailmen would love nothing more than to leap over the dog's fence and wrestle the canine in a no-holds-barred cage match.

What about the last theory? A contemplative man dryly asserts, "It's quite simple, really. Dogs are territorial. Threaten them with illegal passage and they'll bark incessantly, bite if they have to." As with the others, there may be a ring of truth to it, but it, too, falls short. For there are times when a dog is hanging out a car window, wind against his face, and he'll pick me out of a crowd and start going nuts. Even when he's a small dot on the horizon, the distant sound of yapping can still be heard. Do such animals consider the Earth their domain?

No, in all this, there must be a more profound answer, something which can better explain the intense burning within the dog. Now I have to admit that the question has plagued me for quite some time. Solid answers are elusive. And yet, there must be an explanation, for every cause has an effect.

As it stands, here is my view on the matter.

One will observe in nature a number of curious and sometimes frightening traits. Watch a pack of lions feast on some fresh prey. One can almost discern smiles on their faces. But why does the lion so enjoy the taste of the antelope? Consider the praying mantis. After the female mates, she dashes some salt on the poor chap and says, "Bon appétit." Such tragic romance! Why is this? Why does catnip so allure the kitty? Why do bats long for crunchy insects? Why does the pig love to wallow in the mire? All of these distinctive qualities and a thousand more are simply so by natural design. It's just the way they are. And so in like manner, there is an innate, primal, sadistic desire residing within the dog to pounce upon every mailman crossing his path. This craving is as basic as our thirst. Just as the tiger will crouch in the African plains, spying out his prey, waiting to spring into action, so too the dog will devise his own plans of ambush for the mailman. He can do no other. It's as delightful to him as cotton candy is to a child. It's like a drunk's first sip, a gambler's lucky hit, an athlete's victory.

Isaac Watts, the father of English hymnody, wrote, "Let dogs delight to bark and bite, for God hath made them so; let bears and lions growl and fight, for 'tis their nature too."

It's really as simple as that.

I've thought that the Dog Catcher, an emblem of retributive power and justice, might provide a strong enough deterrent for the dog, might curb at least some of its more nefarious intentions. But just as capital punishment will not ultimately deter a depraved man from committing acts of violence, so too my adversary will continue in his criminal ways, even in the face of the Dog Catcher. It is an indisputable fact that creatures follow their greatest desire in any given circumstance. So the threat of death is of little consequence for the dog, if only he can sink his teeth into my milky white legs.

No doubt there are going to be some who find my views extreme or unbalanced, possibly too black and white. And so under the guise of sophistication and nuance these naysayers will have you believe that the dog and the mailman can in fact be friends, so long as there is mutual understanding and honest communication.

One writer in an article on the internet, in a section entitled, "Dog Body Language- Use It! Some Tips for Delivery People" counseled mailmen on how to approach dogs while in their own territory. After discussing the wrong way to approach a dog, which included facing the dog head on and making direct eye contact, traits dominant dogs exploit, she urged the following:

"Non-threatening dogs turn sideways, and look away. They look off into the distance, blink and might even yawn to show how non-threatening they are feeling. At the approach of the more assertive dog, the submissive dog might lower its head or whole body.

As you enter a dog's territory, you should remain passive, stand sideways and look away, blink, maybe even yawn. When introducing yourself to a dog, turn to the side, lower your body, squat, kneel or sit. Don't stare! Look at him out of the corner of your eye, lower your eye lids in a friendly fashion. Extend your hand to the side for him to smell and, if he seems to accept you, scratch under his chin, not over the top of his head."

Look away? Introduce yourself? Sit on the ground? Are you serious? You want me to walk into Brutus' yard and say with a yawn, "Hi there? My name is Austin," and then sit down in front of the one-hundred and eighty pound Rot with lowered eyes? "Here let me scratch under your chin, this nice furry spot under your frothy mouth."

Of course, all of this lying down and head tilting is going to add a considerable amount of time to the route. So I can see it now. My boss calls me into his office and asks, "I've got you thirty-eight minutes over your projected time. What happened out there?" I then begin to demonstrate the new training I received for dealing with dogs, turning my eyes to the side and lowering my body slowly to the ground until I'm on my back, showing my belly as a sign of submission.

"What the hell are you doing, Brown? Get up!"

Or even better, I can imagine lying in a hospital bed with white bandages wrapped around my face. A nurse with a horrified expression leans over and asks, "What happened to you?" I simply yawn, look at her out of the corner of my eye and roll over.

At the end of the day, no amount of psychology or training will be able to fully extinguish that basic desire within the dog to chew on the mailman. But we mailmen quietly accept such things as facts of life. We resign ourselves to this unalterable truth: The dog is our thorn in the flesh. In this respect, the mailman and the cat share a brotherhood that few can fully appreciate or understand.

Chapter 12

The Good, the Bad and the Ugly

"Schools out, schools out, teachers let the monkeys out."

-An old summer chant-

"Kids are nuts, kids are nuts, get'em in school before we beat their butts."

-What most parents are saying about the beginning of August-

The little girl's eyes lit up, and without a moment's hesitation, she ran to the edge of the porch to greet me. Arms extended, fingers wiggling, face marked with joyous expectation, it was evident that she wanted me to hand her the mail.

If you hand the mail to a child who is three or four, you can expect about half of it to make it inside. As they grip it with one hand or pull it close to their chest, hugging it like a teddy bear, letters start slipping out, dribbling all over the place without their least notice. "Mommy, mail. Mommy..." There goes another letter. After about the second time that happens, a mailman wises up and tells the disappointed hatchlings, "Sorry, but I'm going to have to put it in the box." Oftentimes this merely delays the inevitable because of their incredible climbing abilities. But at least it can't be pinned on you.

The little girl standing on the porch looked about seven or eight, old enough to responsibly take the mail inside. So I smiled warmly and delivered the mail into her hands.

She looked well pleased.

The front door suddenly burst open. Two boys came streaking out, shirts off, popsicle stains decorating their faces like Indian war paint.

"Give it here! It's mine!"

The little girl's sweet face contorted into rage, "No, it's mine!"

The first boy out the door, a thin, grungy looking kid, obviously the oldest, commanded his sister to relinquish the goods. As she continued to clutch the mail in a death grip, obviously unwilling to hand it over, he quickly moved past negotiations to brute force.

As the boy yanked on her arm, the girl continued to wildly shout, "It's mine! Mine!"

"Give it here, you got it yesterday! It's my turn!"

"No! (Beginning to cry) No!"

With the situation turning desperate, the little girl resorted to her last defense, a scream of supersonic proportions.

It didn't work. The boy successfully stripped the mail and took off for the front door. His brother, who was up until now nothing more than an excited bystander, shouted, "Let me have some! Let me have some!" And when he realized that his older brother wasn't going to share any of the booty, he tried to tackle him. Once the older boy scored his victory by making it inside, brushing aside his little brother with a push, the younger boy stomped his foot, howled and then began to cry. The two, persecuted siblings, with all the agony and pathos their embittered frames could muster, invoked the name of almighty mom and then ran off in hot pursuit of the villain who robbed them of their postal joy.

There's something about the mail that works children into a frenzy. It's like they turn into ravenous piranhas. If you dangle a fresh piece of meaty junk mail over their heads, they lose all restraint and start snapping uncontrollably. This is especially true towards the end of summer when kids are beginning to turn feral. It's almost as if too much freedom causes them to lose their minds. So for the sake of society they're sent back to school. This not only restores mental health to parents, but it also ushers in a new found silence to the neighborhood. And this pleases the mailman greatly.

Needless to say, children are definitely a factor in mail delivery. One might say that we're kind of like balloons. What child can walk by a balloon without pointing at it, or kicking it, or chasing after it? In the same way, mailmen receive all the affection they could ever want from kids. And then some.

To begin with, children must, in nearly all circumstances, whether far away or close at hand, whether boy or girl, ugly or cute, say "Hi" to the mailman a few dozen times before they feel they've been adequately noticed.

A kid splashing around in a baby pool sees me, raises his hands high into the air and yells out, "Hi, mailman!"

"Hello, there."

This action captures the attention of his two little friends. The one outside the pool, a tan boy kneeling down in the grass, looking at a strange bug crawling across the ground, looks up and exclaims, "Hi, Mr. Mailman!" Having now heard his two buddies greet me, the remaining boy must offer up his own hearty greeting lest he forever remain destitute of happiness.

Now that each has successfully captured the attention of the mailman and has effectively dispensed their hellos, you would think that all would be settled. But not so. By the time the third child utters his happy salutation, the first begins to feel as though his has grown stale. Therefore he revisits the greeting, but this time with more zeal and volume. Naturally the other children can't be outdone, so they begin to sing out with equal fervor.

Trying to keep up with them is a futile endeavor, so the most loving thing I can do is continue to walk away until I'm out of sight. This effectively frees them from their manic fixation and happily reestablishes them in play.

It's really funny when I come across a large group of kids, like what you see when a crowd of daycare children are being led to the park. When one of them catches sight of me and calls out, the whole procession takes interest. All the girls with their little sundresses and ribbons wave to me with happy smiles. For most of the boys, however, they're yelling for the sake of yelling. In fact, it quickly becomes apparent that they aren't even cognizant of what they're saying any longer. They just know that the boy next to them is hopping up and down screaming "Hey, mailman," so they naturally follow suit, spinning and bumping as they go.

Another component to the mailman/child relationship is their insatiable curiosity about who you are and what you're doing. Before I became a letter carrier, I worked at a landscaping business for a short stint. I can remember bouncing along in a truck with my boss while heading out to a job site. We were going to plant some trees at an elementary school. Out of the blue, my boss, who was driving, started to repeat, "What are you doing? Why? What are you doing? Why?" I shot him a perplexed look, but he just continued to stare out the window. No explanation.

When we arrived at the school, recess was in full force. And as we stood at the spot where we were going to plant the trees, shovels in hand, strategy in mind, a boy of about nine years of age wandered over to us.

"What are you doing," began the boy.

"Planting some trees," I said plainly.

"Why?"

"Well," I explained, "The school wants to have some trees out here."

About that time a girl with long blonde hair suddenly appeared.

"What are you doing?"

I was starting to catch on. My boss gave me a knowing look.

As we dug further and further into the hard soil, more and more children became intrigued. Soon a whole assembly of inquisitive kids were asking, "Hey, what are you doing? Why?"

The same is true with the mail. Kids want to know what you're doing on their porch, what that can of mace is on your bag, where you're going, what that can of mace is on your bag, and of course, they want to know why. It's almost as if children start out their lives as miniature scientists. They're full of questions. They're captivated by the mysterious and the foreign, eager to learn more about the wide world around them. For many of these children, such behavior turns out to be quite charming, an innocent curiosity wrapped up in a cute package, even if the sane mind finds it a tad exhausting. But there's another breed of children out there besides the good ones. These are the mad scientists. They too are curious by nature, but they channel their curiosity through entirely different currents. These are the ones that do their research in the mischievous arts of neighborhood terrorism. They like to explore the finer points of environmental destruction, naughtiness, disobedience, deception and all the other forms of bad behavior that can be honed and investigated with youthful glee. Most of the time their energy is directed towards the nerdier kids around them, but once in a while the mailman is forced to deal with these little vagabonds personally.

One of their favorite activities is calling us names. I can remember an occasion when I had to deal with three grungy boys sitting atop a baseball dugout on the west side of my town. One of them, apparently the ringleader of the small group, a fantastically ugly little boy with freckles, watched me approach with growing interest. He had that no-good look on his face, that squinty eyed, "I've got an idea and it ain't nice" kind of look. Under different circumstances, maybe if his friends weren't around, he might have let the idea drift out of his uneducated mind. But his friends were there, so he had an audience and thus felt obligated to start heckling me.

"Look at that dumb lookin' mailman. You suppose he's retarded?"

The other boys started snickering. It was clear that they didn't possess enough courage to engage in this kind of behavior personally, but they were definitely depraved enough to encourage the name calling and enjoy it immensely.

I cast a glance their way but remained stoic.

The boy raised the ante, "I bet I could kick yer ass."

The other boys watched carefully.

"Look at him," suggested the vagrant, "He's scared. I bet he gets beat up by girls."

This last statement caused the boys to begin laughing hysterically. And quite naturally, this kind of positive reinforcement propelled the dirty ringleader to even greater heights. Standing up, he began to make obscene gestures with his crotch, yelling out things unfit for decent ears.

The mature course of action would have been to simply ignore them. But that makes for a boring Saturday afternoon. So I stopped, looked their direction and asked, "How are you girls doing today? Are you enjoying this beautiful afternoon?" And before they could respond, I pulled down my sunglasses slightly and, while peering over the top, said, "Oh, I'm terribly sorry. I thought you were girls playing house up there."

The look on their faces at that moment was well worth every last drop of the fantastically foul language that bombarded me for the next three blocks.

Over the years I have encountered a variety of other naughty children. I can recall an instance on a side street when I turned and noticed a large, white rump sticking out of a car window. Two hands were gripping each cheek, respectively, as the car passed by. The teenagers could be heard hooting and howling with laughter as the one doing the mooning manipulated his rear end in such a manner as to mimic a talking buttock. I think it said, "Hey, mailman!" I frankly found this hilarious.

In addition to being called names, cussed out and mooned, I've had sticky fingers try to steal mail from by bag, snowballs thrown at me, huge bazooka-like squirt guns leveled at me, hoses pointed at my face, and on one occasion, I was even attacked by a mob of dirt bike-riding, cherry-throwing bandits. That was really awkward. My instinct was to mace them, but I didn't. That's frowned upon at the Post Office. So I charged them like a wailing juggernaut, hoping the impressive display of postal fury would frighten them off. Fortunately it worked. It's kind of strange, but years later while playing Texas Hold'em with a group of buddies, this one guy sitting across from me, a young man about nineteen or twenty years old, asked out of the blue, "Hey, aren't you the mailman that I threw some cherries at?" Sure enough, it was one of the cherry grenadiers. From what I've read in police reports since that night, and heard from the mouths of others, it doesn't sound like much has changed since his youthful days. He's still bent on causing trouble.

But of all the children with which I've had to contend, none have quite compared with Andy Barger and Travis Porter, two exceptionally naughty rascals who lived near the Wabash River on City Route 15. They were the modern day equivalents of Huck Finn and Tom Sawyer. Both were full of life, only told the truth when it benefited them, and they both possessed the unique ability of finding trouble anywhere at anytime.

I would often see them along the banks of the river, catching crawdads, throwing rocks, fishing, swimming, doing all the things grubby boys do when they're out exploring. If not there, they could usually be found at a park located along the outskirts of their neighborhood, a small grassy place with one large, bright purple jungle gym. This is where kids from all over congregated to bicker and squeal and generally act like maniacs. Parents call this "burning off energy," but others less acquainted with the ways of children are far more suspicious that something's seriously wrong with their mental health. Either way, this is where the kids went to play.

For Andy and Travis, they liked to dangle and swing high atop the colorful play area, ruling the community of children below like an alpha male might a band of monkeys. From this exalted position they chased off competing boys with sticks, insulted kids passing by on bikes, dared others to perform dangerous stunts, and endlessly teased all the poor girls who wouldn't slug them.

Most of the time, I merely observed their theatrics from a distance, but when I neared Andy's house, I sometimes couldn't avoid a confrontation with their untamed ways.

Here's how it usually went.

Zipping by on their bikes or skidding to a stop right in front of me, they'd say, "Hey, Austin, what's up?"

They apparently knew my name because Andy's mother, an overweight, middle-aged mom with fluffy, blonde hair, always hunted me down each month in order to pick up her SSI check. The boys often traveled along for the ride. So I'm guessing that's where they heard my name.

When asked, "What's up?" I tried to keep my responses brief and smile without displaying any teeth. I'm told that some animals interpret the sight of teeth as a sign of aggression, and I didn't want to take any unnecessary chances.

Andy's mother, nine times out of ten, would be sitting on her porch waiting on the mail.

So with his mom in view, Andy would offer up his services, "Here, let me get the mail."

"Get it, Andy, and bring it here."

Andy would then snatch up the mail and proceed to look through it, not the least bit concerned about his mother, who, by ever increasing degrees, was growing more and more agitated at her son's unwillingness to bring her the mail.   Unable to restrain herself, she would then begin shouting so obscenely loud that flocks of birds would scatter in terror from nearby trees.

Travis would watch the spectacle with growing amusement.

"Andrew Stephen Barger, you bring that mail to me right now!"

Andy would then act like one of the letters wasn't worthy of attention, so he'd hand it to Travis. This would effectively send his mother into a wild fit. Storming off the porch, she would pursue the two fleeing boys with all the industry her unwieldy legs could produce.

When Andy would finally grow bored with the activity, he would give up the mail to his huffing and puffing mother, and then say, with all the practiced charm of a politician, "I'm just teasing, Mom, just teasing. Here ya go."

This is generally how Andy interacted with his mom. He did just about anything he wanted, while his mother, who disapproved of just about everything he did, ushered forth impotent warnings to her seemingly deaf child.

In all the time spent around these two hooligans, I can only recall one major problem that involved me, and amazingly, it only concerned Andy and his much younger brother, a child not known for creating mayhem. My suspicion is that Travis was in fact involved but avoided detection. Whatever the case, it all began when I rounded the corner of the last block of relay thirteen. As I approached my truck from the back, I noticed that Andy and his little brother were suddenly walking away from the front of my truck, hands in pocket. Something felt off, so I called out, "Hey, Andy! What ya up to?"

He turned around and gave me a very polished, bored look. Something was definitely up. As they continued on their way, I turned to investigate my truck.

Let's see here. Nothing on the grill. Headlights: check. No dents. Tires... hello, what's this? Situated right in front of my tire, balanced on its head, was a large nail, the tip barely touching the rubber.

"Hey, Andy!"

He turned around again. His face looked concerned.

"Hey, come here. I want to ask you something."

He hesitated. Knowing a thing or two about the minds of little boys, I could see that he was mulling over his options. He was trying to decide between flight or denial. He went with the latter.

"What's wrong, Austin?"

I held up the nail.

He shrugged his shoulders.

His younger brother hadn't yet fully matured in the skills of deception, so his face bore the evidence of guilt. That, in addition to his standing perfectly still, and as rigid as a two by four, solidified my suspicions.

"Did you put the nail under my truck?"

"No... No, I didn't."

"Are you sure?"

"Positive."

"Then how," I asked with a severe look, "did it get there?"

He shrugged again.

I asked his brother of about five years of age the same questions. Amazingly, the little guy held his ground and continued to plead innocence. He was apparently more skilled than I had anticipated.

I felt stumped. They weren't wavering in the least, and it seemed that anything short of torture wouldn't get the truth out of them.

That's when I saw it.

Sitting about four feet away from my truck, resting on the grass, was an empty box of nails. I considered it for a moment and then got an idea. Walking over, I carefully picked it up by one of the corners, tweezer-like, and said, "You see this box, boys? It's got your fingerprints all over it. That's right. The police are going to know it was you who planted these nails. So look, you'd better fess up now. Tell me the truth. You don't want them coming to your house to arrest you, do you?"

That worked. They broke down and confessed their sins with all the penitence and shame of a burdened saint, swearing that their tender hearts had at that moment been fully rehabilitated by the pains of sorrow. I interrupted their mournful pleadings and asked, "How many nails did you plant underneath cars?"

"Maybe twenty."

"*Twenty!?!*"

I told the boys to go home immediately and tell their mother what they had done and then to go back out and collect all the nails.

"You're going to get into huge trouble if you pop someone's tire," I warned with an extended finger.

With that, they ran off, sobbing audibly.

Twenty nails? I thought to myself, glancing over at a red pickup truck across the street. I could see a nail under the front tire. It was Dan Parker's truck, a guy who absolutely adores his vehicles. The last automobile you would ever want to mess with would be Dan Parkers. When the PT Cruiser first came out he bought one, cherry red, and loved that thing with all the affection a man can produce- carefully wiping it down with white towels, caressing it while waxing, even hugging it from time to time.

Oh yeah, he'll call the cops for me.

Needless to say, when I showed him the nail and told him where I found it, something deep within him flared, and a moment later he called the cops.

I decided to go and see whether the two boys did in fact go home. Of course, they didn't. I found them about three blocks from their house, walking casually along as though they hadn't a care in the world. When I pulled over next to them, they looked surprised to see me.

"What are you guys doing here?" I asked in astonishment. "The police are heading to your house right now. They're looking for you. Run! Run home now! You hear me? Run!"

Boy, did they run.

When I swung back around their way to drop off some parcels, I was actually a little surprised to see a cop at their house. I could see their mom outside, hugging her two boys, pulling them in close, imploring the policeman to have mercy on her repentant delinquents.

"Oh, I'll make sure they'll never do anything like this again, officer," I heard her say in a convincing tone. "I'll take away their

Game Boy. The TV. I'll take away everything for a month. Don't worry. I'll make sure they get it, officer." And then she hugged them again.

The cop appeared satisfied and drove off.

I couldn't believe it. That red handed sinner had somehow escaped from the clutches of the police with nothing more than a slap on the wrist. I was at least hoping to see a good flogging. But, no, Tom Sawyer prevailed yet again. Before I could say "Brag to your friends" he was lying along the banks of the river relaxing and fishing with Travis Porter soaking up the sun without a care in the world.

Chapter 13

Goldtooth

You have about a 1 in 5,000 chance of being struck by lightning, if
you live to be 80 years old.
You have a 1 in 649,740 chance of being dealt a royal flush.
You have about a 1 in 729,000 chance of having quadruplets
(naturally).

––––––––––––––––––––

My thoughts were interrupted by a car that suddenly pulled
over next to me. Mrs. Mosley rose from the vehicle with a jubilant
smile, hair all fixed up in wondrous knot, attire surprisingly neat
and tidy.

"Hey, Baby!" announced the woman with a voice that
benefitted the whole of society.

It may seem strange to the reader, given the rather
unpleasant parting that graced our initial acquaintance in chapter
three, that Mrs. Mosley would now greet me so warmly. The reason
for this is a matter of curious forgetfulness on her part.

After Goldtooth sped off in her car, the next time I met
her was at the little old lady's house, the one you may recall with the
twitching lips and grey spasmodic hair who occupied shotgun.
While making my way up Jefferson Avenue, I could just make out
the two of them from a distance occupying a tiny, largely grassless
front lawn. Both were sitting casually in some yellow folding chairs.

Mrs. Mosley, when she caught scent of my approach, called
out in a charismatic voice, "Hey there, mailman! How's it goin'?" I
wasn't quite sure what to make of the cheerful promotion, but I
decided to play along and act like we were old buds. I soon found
that we were conversing together with great freedom and ease, our
posture and tone entirely free from any hint that something
disturbing had ever transpired between us. In fact, Mrs. Mosley felt
so at ease with my present company that she found a request for

some spare money to be an effortless application of friendly chatter. The appeal began with a glance towards the little old lady, "Hey now, you don't suppose I could borrow money for a stamp, do ya?" This was followed by a forward motion, a lean of sorts, which suggested confidentiality. "It's for Iris." With that she gave a none-too-subtle tilt of the head towards the dear old woman. I looked over at her. She shot me a serene smile.

As I trust you can imagine, I wasn't entirely prepared to be hit up for money, and the soft tug of manipulation was causing my spidey senses to tingle. But when I actually considered turning down an elderly woman's desire to "borrow" thirty some odd cents, words like 'stingy' and 'Grinch' crept in my mind. So I thought, *Oh what's the hurt in it?* and proceeded to dig around for some loose change.

It would have been nearly impossible for me to understand the implications of dropping a few coins into her hand, but that one seemingly benign act proved to be a magical moment for Mrs. Mosley. In the twinkling of an eye, I was no longer viewed as merely a mailman, but as a piggy bank that, when properly shaken, would dispense shiny coins into her outstretched hand. The reader should note that this transformation had the effect of securing, for all eternity, a congenial spirit in the heart of Mrs. Mosley towards me. And so this explains in large part why Mrs. Mosley, having presently exited the car next to me, could greet me so affectionately.

With this cleared up, we're almost ready to continue the story. But I first need to point out a few other important details. It should be understood that the time between my first encounter with Mrs. Mosley, and the greeting which begins this chapter, constitutes a space of five years. This means that there had been ample time for her to jiggle the piggy bank. And more importantly, it means that I've had plenty of experience in dealing with Mrs. Mosley, and that I thereby feel qualified to say a thing or two about this winsome, and yet, very wily woman.

Mrs. Mosley, though on the plump side, can oftentimes be found walking the streets in search of a friend's house or grocery store. Her manner of walking has a hint of regality to it, a certain sense of owning the very sidewalk under her feet. But this is diminished greatly by the slight waddle that complicates her stride.

She prefers extravagant clothing, especially those outfits which detail a leopard pattern somewhere within a general scheme of otherwise brilliant colors, as well as a red, paisley handkerchief for head covering. Sometimes the handkerchief is exchanged for something that looks like a broad sweat band, which, when wrapped tightly around her head, causes her hair to sprout out the top like a piece of broccoli.

Mrs. Mosley, as the title suggests, is married to a Mr. Mosley. He's a tall, lanky, bending man with short curly hair whose eyes, though tinged with yellow, are like a pair of passive monks in deep meditation. He considers words burdensome or unnecessary, secondary forms of communication to that of the rumbling affirmative, "Mmmmhuh." His head bobs slowly in agreement as he hums his slow confirmation, though the bobbing will increase in its rapidity if you happen to touch upon a subject that fancies him. In contradistinction to his wife, Mr. Mosley prefers bland colors, often earth tones, especially those of the late 70's, and apparently considers walking, or leaving his house for that matter, an evil to be avoided at great lengths. Therefore, I have seen very little of the man and am unable to say much more about him besides the general observation that he appears to be in poor health.

In order to better comprehend the character of Mrs. Mosley, it needs to be understood that while she can be quite charming and humorous, the light conversation that often passes between her and her audience is often nothing more than a preamble, a short step towards the greater objective, which is a request to "borrow" some money. It took a while for me to realize this, but Mrs. Mosley is a moocher *par excellence*.

In my earlier dealings with the woman, she would meander up to my truck, or bump into me while walking a relay, and maneuver a casual conversation around to asking for some "change." I'm putting the word "change" in quotes because her idea of change ranged from fifty cents to ten dollars- ten dollars hardly being spare change by my standards. As I would naturally inquire into her reasons for needing some "change," she might explain, after much hem-hawing and coughing, that some Sammy guy needed a few dollars. Pressing further, Mrs. Mosley would reluctantly confess that he needed some smokes. A raised eyebrow, in conjunction with a screwed up face, elicited the following, "Now don't chew-be like that! Come on, now. Sammy needs some smokes. What's a few dollars for Sammy?"

Being a woman greatly gifted in the art of obsecration, Mrs. Mosley soon learned that if she appealed for money in the name of her ailing husband, I would be far more prone to open my wallet. So on one occasion, she convinced me that he needed a few dollars for public transportation; to the hospital, of course. I didn't have cash on me, just plastic, so I said that I'd swing by her house after work and help her out. Later that evening when I showed up with the funds, a young man in his late teens answered the door. Behind him, in a room packed with family and friends, a dozen heads turned and regarded me with strange looks. When, and much to her surprise, Mrs. Mosley saw that it was me, she quickly stepped outside, pulled the door shut and gratefully received my money. I knew I had been tricked, but didn't raise a fuss. I was fine with giving her the money, even if it was probably going to be used for a movie rental. My thinking was that maybe, just maybe, some measure of guilt might play on her conscience and lead to a change in behavior. But no. Mrs. Mosley remained firmly established in her ways.

So I trust you can understand, dear reader, why I was feeling something less than joy when Mrs. Mosley suddenly emerged from the stopped car. In spite of my inward murmurings, I responded to her jovial salutation with a cheerful, "Hey, what's up?"

"Fine day, isn't it?" She asked while looking around at the unextraordinary weather.

"Yeah, I suppose so."

I noticed some papers in her hand. My guess was that she needed a stamp or an envelope.

She caught my gaze and asked, "You know where I'm going?"

"Uh, no, where?"

"I'm gonna get my pitcha taken."

"Your picture, huh?"

"Yep, that's right."

By this point, I couldn't help but notice just how nice she looked, with respect to her usual standards, anyway. There were no crazy colors detailing her dress or strange apparatuses hanging from her neck, and I think she was wearing makeup. Many would still find her choice of style questionable, but on the whole, she looked nice.

"You know why I'm gonna get my pitcha taken?"

I shook my head.

She unfolded the papers. As she did this, she spoke in an even, controlled tone, "You know how the lotto people will set up over by the drug store? Well, I won som'in."

I glanced down and saw a paper that looked like an oversized check. In a box off to the right, I saw the following figure: $33,000.00.

"Whoa! You won 33,000 dollars!" I exclaimed.

She shook her head and motioned for me to look again, this time with her finger pointing to something typed out towards the top of the check. It read: 1 of 30.

My look showed that I didn't understand, but she didn't say anything. She allowed me a moment to ponder the implications. And then, all at once, I began to comprehend its significance. That was the first of thirty such checks. Goldtooth had hit big.

"It's close to a million dollars." She said.

A million dollars. Yep, that's right. Mrs. Mosley had apparently won a million bucks, and as she was heading off for a photo shoot, saw me and decided to pull over and share the good news.

Cruel ironies began to form in my mind, as I thought about her winning that much money. Stupefied, I asked, "Wow, so what now? What are you going to do with the money?"

At this, Mrs. Mosley spoke of visiting family out in California, vacationing abroad, and throwing a killer party or two. I noticed that the word "give" didn't find its way into her spending itinerary, so I thought I would ask if she had thought about giving some away to charity. With a dexterous change of tone she proclaimed, "Oh, yes. I'm gonna give something to the Church- one can't forget God, ya know. Mmmmhuh, gotta give some to God, and..." And from here, Mrs. Mosley gained momentum until she crested the upper heights of generosity, proclaiming with great conviction and enthusiasm all the good that would be accomplished. I may be wrong, but I think I detected the faint outline of an angelic halo over her head, as she continued to spell out her altruistic plans.

I showed my approval by nodding my head with round eyes, while secretly harboring a fleet of suspicions about her sincerity. I mean really, could that which is called the root of evil suddenly convert Mrs. Mosley into an orphan-supporting, hospital-erecting, philanthropist? Could it be that this much money would awaken the Mother Teresa within her, which, up to this point, had been merely slumbering in a dormant state?

After pausing for a moment to catch her breath, she began her prophecies afresh, but now with an eye on my own awards, "Now don't you worry," she began with a reassuring look, "I'm gonna give you and Jerry a little somethin' special, seein' how you've been so good to me over the years."

I showed my surprise and smiled slightly, breathing, "Oohh, uh, thanks."

With that Mrs. Mosley gave me a big hug, bid me farewell, and left for her photo shoot.

I'm thinking that the "special somethin" must be really amazing, since it hasn't arrived yet. She must be putting a lot of thought into it or possibly traveling great distances to find it. Shoot, maybe she's just preoccupied with relief work in Darfur? It's hard to say. But don't you worry, Mrs. Mosley, Jerry and I are still eagerly awaiting the arrival of that wonderful gift you have planned for us. In the meantime, you don't suppose you could pay me back for all those stamps you've borrowed, do you?

Chapter 14

Storms

"We've been through every kind of rain there is. Little bitty stinging rain and big old fat rain, rain that flew in sideways, and sometimes rain even seemed to come straight up from underneath."

-Forrest Gump-

"Neeeeeeeeeeeeeeeeeeeeeeeeeee.
(A pause followed by some clicking sounds)
The National Weather Service has issued a severe thunderstorm warning for..."

-NWS-

I looked at the rain gear in the back of my truck, considered the growing darkness out to the west, and then looked at the rain gear again. A storm was building, and I couldn't decide whether to go ahead and put on my rain gear or try to fit in another relay before it cut loose.

Mailmen often struggle with this decision. That's because raingear, besides perhaps burlap underwear, is the single most heinously uncomfortable article of clothing known to mankind. For when you slide on a poncho, it's like you're instantly transported to the upper regions of the Mojave Desert. It's thought that for every thirty minutes a mailman wears all his rain gear, a full day is subtracted from his lifespan. I'm convinced that there have even been some who have suffered brain damage from wearing it too long. I mean really, the evidence is everywhere.

There's also the Herculean task of trying to stretch a pair of rubber galoshes over our shoes. Like some kind of event in a strong man competition, we chalk our hands and pull and strain until our eyes bulge.

And we can't forget about those sexy pith helmets either. Few things engender more pointing and laughing or silly comments than pith helmets. "Out on an African safari, mailman?" someone asks with a chuckle. Or, "Whatcha got on yer head, mailman? A flying saucer?"

On the flip side, the choice to forego raingear can mean becoming acquainted with a misery of a different sort. It only takes about a minute of walking in a hard rain before your clothes stick to your skin and you're afforded the pleasure of experiencing that wondrously icky, wet shirt feeling. Water also dribbles down your head and then down your neck, finds a path along your back, accumulates around the waist, locates a gap and then adventures afresh lower and lower until it pools at the bottom of your shoe. And when your shoes get wet, it's all over, for each step becomes a gushy, mushy, skin rubbing movement that makes your little piggies squeal with discomfort.

Most porches also have an assortment of drips and waterfalls running off the front edge, usually right in the middle of the steps leading up to the mailbox. Without raingear, only the exceedingly agile can slip between these mini-Niagaras or jump through them quickly enough so as to avoid getting drenched. It's often a futile endeavor though. More times than not, by the time a carrier makes it back to his truck, he's a goner, and no amount of raingear can resuscitate his comfort.

So on that sultry midsummer afternoon while standing at the back of my truck, this was the delicate choice facing me: Put on raingear, or leave it behind? By my estimation, I had about a 50% chance of getting nailed if I chose to go without raingear.

While tapping the truck with my fingers, I continued to eye the western horizon. A black mass was slowly overtaking the blue skies. It didn't look good at all. *Ah, I can make it,* I thought to myself, as I threw the mailbag over my shoulder. *Yeah, I can beat it.* And with that, I set off at a brisk pace, choosing to play chicken with the approaching storm.

There's something awesome and thrilling and terrifying about the approach of a storm. It doesn't matter how many I walk through, I experience the same exquisite feelings of anxiety and excitement each time. As the wind builds and the trees begin to rustle with growing dismay, as children run up and down the sidewalks with renewed energy, smiling and leaping amid swirling papers, as people adorn their porches and chatter and point and resurrect stories of forgotten storms, as the lightening cracks and the thunder responds with a peel, I feel a sense of anticipation welling within me. I feel alive. I feel scared. These are the preliminary notes- the storm's tuning up- preceding nature's furious symphony. And mailmen experience every last drop of it. We witness nature's awful beauty in its most raw form, unshielded and face-to-face.

Soon the sun was snuffed out like a candle, and a grim shadow fell across the landscape, leaving me with a sense of eerie stillness. With about two blocks to go before I would make it back to my truck, I became concerned, not so much about getting caught in a downpour, though that still registered in my mind, but because the sky had a strange greenish-yellow hue to it.

While growing up, my brother and I were thoroughly educated by our mother about severe weather. She did this by feeding us a healthy dose of TV programs with titles like "When Tornadoes Strike!" or "It Sounded like a Freight Train." My mother, having grown up around trailer homes, and having been terrified by the thought of a nader making her mobile home live up to its name, felt it was her duty to acquaint us with every weather program that aired in the month of April. And so having seen nearly every imaginable video recording of skies that produce tornadoes, my trained eye found some alarming parallels between what I had seen on TV and what was now churning above me. But I still wasn't terribly concerned, that is, until I heard the siren start up.

I wouldn't say that I was instantly catapulted into a state of panic, but that wailing siren certainly tugged on the one thread still holding my cool composure together. Let's just say that if you happened to be one of the concerned people watching the sky out their window, you would have seen me trotting down the sidewalk, head wheeling, eyes like two pith helmets. I don't care how hardened someone is, there's something unnerving about a tornado siren, especially when there's a funky colored storm swirling overhead.

Soon the trees were swaying violently, as strong gusts of wind ripped through their leafy branches. It felt as if each tree were frantically waving its arms, warning, "Faster, mailman! It's coming! You need to move faster!" And so I went faster. There then followed a low rumble that could be heard building until it finally exploded in a great crescendo, as if a hundred black powder canons had been fired off in succession.

The last house on the relay was an old Victorian home with three wide steps leading up to an airy porch. When I shut the lid to that box, the first drops of rain could be heard pelting against the ground. So in a final dash, I ran to my truck, flung open the door and hurled myself inside.

"Ha-ha! I made it!" I announced triumphantly. But just barely. Seconds later, a torrential rain cut loose.

As the storm beat furiously against my truck, I noticed that there were small chunks of ice bouncing off my windshield. Naturally, I knew that this was another sign of potential tornadic activity. So this, in conjunction with the wind whistling through the cracks of my truck, as well as the siren that continued to scream in the distance, and the serrated lines of light that streaked across the ominous sky, all these, I say, were sufficient indications that I needed to seek shelter and fast. But where? I was parked in the middle of a residential area, so my options were severely limited. Mrs. Lancaster, an elderly woman who lived just up the way, would no doubt gladly invite me into her home, but I had no idea if she had a basement. I certainly didn't want to die while huddled up in her bathroom next to an avocado-green toilet. So the only other option was the Catholic school around the corner.

In this scenario, I envisioned a throng of elementary kids all lined up in the hallway, tucked up into tiny balls, faces down, hands on top of their heads. I then wondered if the principal would expect me to do the same. Such a prospect didn't thrill me, but after a moment's deliberation, I decided about anything would be better than my present location. So I cast my lot with the Catholic school.

A few moments later, I entered through the front door and found myself standing in a dim lobby. A large mural of Jesus teaching little children figured prominently in the spacious entry.

Looking around, commotion buzzed everywhere. Teachers with waving arms were filing children to predetermined tornado safety zones, their voices loud, though still plenty sweet. Some of the adults were obviously hiding their anxiety behind forced smiles as their students carelessly plodded along, each following the kid in front of them, some talking and laughing, others bouncing off their buddies with exaggerated jolts, and not a few girls shuffling their feet with sober expressions.

I stood motionless amid the fray and considered my options. One of the teachers who was herding her class into the boy's bathroom caught my attention and bid me to come on in with them. I nodded gratefully and joined the march.

It wasn't until then that I realized the power was out. Entering the bathroom, therefore, meant walking into a very dark space. The only source of light was what entered through the propped door, which was partially obscured by the outline of the teacher who was still herding kids inside.

Soon about thirty, neatly uniformed boys and girls were sitting in the middle of a decent smelling restroom, with me squatting down, only a few feet from a urinal, feeling like an ogre surrounded by halflings. I was the object of considerable intrigue and could see their blinking eyes through the darkness.

I offered a friendly wave to my onlookers. A little boy near me waved back.

The teacher came and knelt down amongst the uneasy group. Looking my way, she asked in a lighthearted tone, "So you decided to come join us today? Good to have you, mailman."

I smiled in return, adding with excitement, "Yeah, it's *nasty* out there! You should see the sky. Seriously, it's kinda yellow and green, definitely made me think tornado. Never seen it so bad, so I thought I'd better find some shelter just in case. And *the wind...*"

By the time the word 'wind' left my mouth, I noticed that the woman was shooting me an eloquent look. Her eyes expanded and then darted around the room, eyebrows lifting with each quick movement. As she did so, her head tilted to one side, twitching slightly. Since it was dark, it was hard for me to understand what she was doing. But when I did, I caught my voice and looked around at the thirty little white faces staring at me through the darkness, each motionless and looking as if they had seen a ghost.

"Oh..."

I tried my best to recover, "But uh, well, no, I've certainly seen worse. Yeah, definitely. There's definitely nothing to be afraid of. In fact, I bet this..." And on I went, trying to sound confident and reassuring. I even craned my neck towards the door at one point as if I were trying to catch a glimpse of the sun, which I supposed to be on the verge of popping out.

By the looks of the children, I was providing little comfort, and so I talked a bit more and then clamped my rambling mouth shut. The teacher didn't say anything. Actually, no one did. We sat there in the dark and waited the storm out.

It ended up that there weren't any tornados. Just a lot of rain. The only real damage came from my poorly chosen words. I'm hoping that a few months of counseling from Fr. Mitchell will help heal the emotional scars.

Sorry, kids.

Well, fortunately, I've never seen a real live tornado while walking the mail. Once I was sequestered in a hospital because somebody supposedly saw one about thirteen miles away in the middle of a field. So far as I know, that's the closest I've ever been to a twister, though that's apparently close enough to set things into high alert at the hospital.

"It's headed straight for us," announced a pale-faced administrator who looked like she was about to lose it.

All the people in our particular wing were instructed to stand in the hallway. Everyone from patients, to nurses, to guys in lab coats holding vials of fluids in these things that looked like crates with handles, were packed into a long hallway like letters in a case. I was standing next to an older man in a wheel chair who wanted to tell me about his days of flying during the Vietnam War. The stories were interesting enough, except he kept stopping mid-sentence and elbowing me, intending for me to look over at one of the nurses whom he thought looked "real pretty." "What we got here?" he kept saying with a sneaky grin. I didn't pay him too much attention, because the administrator, who was as white as ever and fidgeting nervously, looked like she could pass out at any moment. A few nurses got her to calm down and that pretty much ended the show.

While it's true that I've never seen a real tornado, I have seen storms that, at the time, I would have sworn were destined to produce one. I can vividly remember standing on a sidewalk looking straight up into the most terrifying mass of clouds I've ever seen. It was an awful beauty. Great undulating mountains of grey and black rolled across the sky, a sky that seemed to be breathing, living, animated by a life-force of its own. An immense bulge swelled and churned directly overhead, as if the finger of the Almighty were stirring a dark cauldron. It crept downward and rotated ever so slowly. At that moment I felt hopelessly small and fragile, like an insect before the mouth of a great furnace. My thoughts were driven to ponder heavenly realities. I thought of the future judgment and how God, in all His holy wrath, would exceed the strength and terror of that storm by infinite degrees; how the storm could swallow me whole without the slightest effort; and then how God, in His divine omnipotence, will dwarf the unrighteous and stop their mouths. Oh, how terrible it will be for some on that day.

I'm not the first to have been moved by the approach of a coming storm. Carl Boberg, while strolling through the beautiful coastlands of southeast Sweden, was suddenly caught in a midday thunderstorm. The flashing violence of the storm, in addition to the brilliant sun and chirping birds that followed the fierce episode, prompted the man to fall to his knees in humble adoration of his awesome God. As a result, he soon pinned a Swedish poem that has come to be known today as the hymn, "How Great Thou Art." The first line reads thus:

"O Lord my God, when I in awesome wonder, consider all the worlds Thy Hands have made; I see the stars, I hear the rolling thunder, Thy power throughout the universe displayed. Then sings my soul, my Savior God, to Thee, how great Thou art, how great Thou art."

I once witnessed something similar near a lumber yard. A huge funnel cloud was descending to the earth, black, thick and growing steadily. The scene astonished me so greatly that I ran inside to tell everyone to come out and take a look. Moments later, several of us were standing in the parking lot watching in wonder as this thing made its way across our town, hovering in that partially descended state for what seemed like an eternity. One of the lumber yard employees spoke to the storm, "Come on down, baby. Let's see what you got. Let's see it." That was easy for him to say, since it was moving away from us.

Indiana certainly has its fair share of thunderstorms and averages around twenty tornadoes per year. But the most common form of foul weather, and what is downright miserable for mailmen, has to be the innumerable grey skies that leak rain for hours on end. Off and on. Off and on, they go. Just about the time we put away our pith helmets and take off our galoshes, the rain starts up again.

When there's a steady shower, little can be done for the mail. We try to cover it with a flap on our mailbag, one designed to protect the mail, but it has a profound limitation. You have to move it in order to get at the mail. So what this means is that the mail towards the end of the relay gets soaked and sticks together like a bunch of paper-thin magnets. Then the ink rubs off on your fingers, sometimes taking the address with it. And before long we're looking down at a worn out letter asking, "Now whose was this?"

Then there's the dreaded door slot. While trying to slide a soggy catalog through a two-inch opening, it gets caught on a microscopic lip and bends to a stop. Now matter how delicately one tries to slide it through, no matter how many different angles are adopted, that little lip catches the catalog every time, saying, "No, sir, try again. Nope, ha-ha, try again," in much the same way that a pop machine, no matter how smooth you make the money, won't accept the bill. After a number of failed attempts, the sliding motion is abandoned for the more satisfying action, the cram, or shove. So if any of you who own a door slot have ever wondered why your mail is mutilated, well, now you know.

After a long day of slopping around in the rain, mailmen come walking back into the post office thoroughly disgruntled, hair drenched, shirts dark with the stain of water. We peel off our rain gear and throw it down in mute disgust. "Splat!" Most of the clerks are smart enough to leave us alone, though a few try to cheer us up by greeting us warmly. It's just about then when a pot-bellied carrier comes strolling over to the time clock to check back in from the street, his shirt and shoes completely dry, right arm slightly moist. It's Bill, a carrier whose years of seniority have earned him a route wholly delivered from the comfort of his truck. He considers our wet forms, and then, with a face like that of a man who has caught the scent of something delicious, announces, "Man, I hate it when my right arm gets chilled by the rain." Those of us who are soaked groan and secretly envy the dry mailman, wishing with all our hearts that we too could crack the same, stupid joke.

Chapter 15

"Hawaii, the most sought-after postal route of them all, where the air is so dewy-sweet you don't even have to lick the stamps."

-Newman-

My hesitating fingers searched for the perfect words as they hovered over the keyboard. It seemed to me that everything hinged upon the right phraseology, but so little could be said in the space of a few sentences. How in the world could I make the phrase "Looking for a mutual transfer to North Carolina from a small town in central Indiana" glamorous and inviting when there really wasn't anything glamorous or inviting about it? I could imagine someone from the Tar Heel State pulling out a map, muttering "Where's that?" and then, after finally locating my city, the little dot smack dab in the middle of obscurity, cracking, "Good luck, man." But could I blame them? Most people aren't looking to move to a flat, corn-filled, humid summer, cold winter, run-of-the-mill, Indiana town. But regardless of the chances, I had to go for it.

For mailmen, there's something called a mutual transfer that allows carriers to exchange job locations with another individual if both parties are willing to swap. It's a pretty awesome opportunity when you stop to think that you can move virtually anywhere in the United States if you can just find a person willing to take the plunge. But that's of course the catch. You have to find somebody who wants to switch. And what are the odds that someone who sunbathes nearly every day in California is going to open the Postal Record or look on PostalMag.com, two places where people post their transfer requests, and say, "Carrie, look! Someone from the land of 'all the leaves are brown and the sky is grey' is willing to come out to sunny California and take my place." Not likely. But again, one has to try, right?

And so once I finished my "Shakespearian" advertisement and paid the fifteen dollar fee to have it listed in the Postal Record, I eagerly waited for the calls to come pouring in.

It didn't take long before one of the guys at work noticed my listing. With a clear, resonating voice for all to hear, he announced, "Brown's trying to move to North Carolina! Ha-ha-ha-ha. Hey, did you lie about how beautiful it is around here? Did you tell'em we have beaches? Mwaa-ha-ha-ha." That initiated an avalanche of heckles. Carriers all around me were covering their mouths, trying to restrain laughter. Voices declaring, "You aren't going anywhere," or, "What moron would actually come here?" could be heard echoing throughout the workroom floor. There were even two carriers who, knowing with delicious certainty that they would never be summoned for the task, promised, "We'll help ya move, won't we, Jim?" "Oh, yeah, don't you worry, we'll be right over when it's time to pack ya up, man." But amid all the jeers and chuckles and proclamations about how stupid someone would have to be to move to Dullville, I continued to cling to the fact that I didn't need six, or three, or even two, but I only needed one moron to say, "Rural Indiana? Sure, let's give that a try."

My sons were once asked by their mom, "What would you do if you were hungry and had nothing to eat?"

Calvin, my son of seven replied, "I would pray."

Ethan, age five, asked, "Well, am I in the desert or in the jungle? If I'm in the desert, I would pray. If I'm in the jungle, I'd find something to eat."

Neither response was bad, really. And in my situation, I needed to do just that. I needed to hunt and pray. I needed to take the bull by the horns and look to God. So even though I had become an object of ridicule, it felt good to take action, for I was a man trying to escape from the ghettos of Indiana weather, a man trusting in God's good providence to provide a way out. And so I sat back and waited. And I waited some more.

Time continued to roll by.

And then more time...

And more time...

I'd like to say that I finally received that one, magical phone call that enabled me to move to North Carolina, where I ended up writing this chapter from a breezy vista overlooking the Atlantic. But I can't. The one and only phone call I received came from some guy down in Raleigh.

7:00 am. Phone rings.

"Hello."

"Hi, is this the carrier looking to transfer to North Carolina?"

"Why, yes. Yes it is. Are you thinking about coming to Indiana?"

"Well, uh, no. Not really. Well, maybe."

"Okay..."

"What are the schools like?"

(I explain what our schools are like).

"What kind of commerce do you have up there?"

"Commerce?"

"Yeah."

(I talk about our corn.)

"Anything else?"

"Um, beans."

"I see."

"Oh, and there are different manufacturing plants."

"What are the housing costs like up there?"

"Oh, very good. Some of the lowest in the nation."

"Well, see, that's my problem. Houses are really expensive down here."

"I've heard that. Thinking about moving somewhere more affordable?"

"Well... I don't think so. Well, maybe."

"Um, ok."

"My daughter and I moved into this one house in Raleigh and..." (Enter life story here.)

Basically, the man from Raleigh wanted to chat.

As the days turned into weeks and then into months, I began to slowly accept my destiny.

In a last ditch effort, I considered one more option. A mailman can transfer to another office if (1) there's an opening, and (2) they're willing to lose all their seniority and start out fresh as a mere PTF[2]. But there has to be something wrong with a mailman's head, if he'll actually consider giving up his regular status for that kind of transfer.

Since I wasn't willing to go that route, I was pretty much stuck in Indiana. But curiosity, nevertheless, drove me to look at potential PTF openings. So I fired up the computer and took a look around. Here's what I found.

North Carolina: Zero openings.

Florida: One opening (but probably already taken).

Texas: Zero openings.

Hawaii: ROFL.

Do you want to know how many openings were available in Indiana? Fifty three.

I didn't want to interpret that as a bad sign, but it wasn't very promising. My guess is that nearly every mailman above 40 degrees N latitude has their eyes fixed on these states and are likewise clamoring for a transfer to one of these spots, offering complimentary incentives like organ donations.

So what now? I guess God has a plan for me in Indiana for the time being. But then again, maybe the right moment just hasn't come along yet. So how about one last shameless advertisement:

Letter Carrier looking to transfer to anywhere warm. I live in a gorgeous and extremely exciting small town in Indiana, an enchanting place where you'll experience all the wonders of each amazing season. Please contact Austin Brown if you are interested.

Thank you.

---

[2] Chapter eighteen will explain what the term PTF means. Until then, all you need to know is that a PTF is a crappy, no seniority, entry position that only people with masochistic tendencies enjoy.

Chapter 16

Mac and Me

"One of the great benefits of living in a civilized society is that we don't have to live with animals in our homes."

-The more seasoned perspective of my wife-

My four year old son exclaimed, "Let's call him Mac!"

I stood in my kitchen looking down at our newly acquired dog whose name was now Mac. How it got to this point was still a question that was very much unresolved in my mind. It's no secret that I have my, shall we say, reservations about that class of animal called the dog. So as I trust you can imagine, I was more than a little reluctant to provide quarters to the furry critter. But here he was. Yes, there he stood, in the middle of my kitchen, both of my boys squatting in front of him, petting him, stroking him, getting in his face too much and doing all of the things that little boys do when they get a new dog. And there stood my wife, across from me, eyes beaming as she watched her sons play and giggle with Mac.

I'm not sure what my expression was like at that moment, but I tend to think that I was smiling one of those smiles that we try to sustain when a host gives us a large plate of liver or tuna or maybe brussel sprouts. Sure, you chew and smile, even nod your head as if to say, "Oh, yummy, thank you," but in reality you're trying to choke back your gag reflex and camouflage the tears that are forming in your eyes. So whether I liked it or not, I had to swallow the fact that I was now the owner of a small, adult, grey terrier.

In my mind there seemed to be an intimate connection between the acquisition of Mac and another dog, a Mr. Beagle, of long ago. Early on in our marriage, when we were young and something like pups ourselves, my wife would subtly drop hints about wanting a baby by saying, "I want a baby now." At that point in my immature life, I didn't feel ready for that kind of responsibility, so in an attempt to muffle the ticking of her biological clock she went after the next best thing, a dog. I felt a little reluctant to get one- I was a mailman back then- but figured that a puppy would buy me at least a year in the baby department, so I didn't make too much of a fuss. Needless to say, we decided to get a puppy.

As she left for the pound with her partner in crime, my mom, I made one simple request, "Oh, hey, don't get a beagle, ok? Anything but a beagle." Those dogs quite possibly have the most annoying bark on the planet, and so I cringed at the thought of having to listen to some dumb beagle howl each and every time company stopped by.

So what did she come home with? Yep, that's right. A beagle.

"Austin, it was the only cute puppy there. There weren't any other good options... I know, I know, but it'll grow on you. Trust me. Just give it some time."

Well, he was adorable in his own doggy kind of way, but his cuteness was obscured by a malfunction of sorts. This beagle had one of the most incredible poopers I had ever seen. No, seriously. I'm fully aware that dogs have to do their duty, but this pup had super canine powers in that department. He could empty at least half his body weight out of his rear, and quite naturally, this fantastic quantity would be dispensed somewhere on our living room carpet.

Bek had read somewhere that if you put a dog in a crate at night they will refrain from pooping in it until morning. According to the article, they wouldn't want to sleep in their doo doo. But alas, our puppy had apparently never read that article. Every morning at about 5:30 a.m., we'd hear Mr. Beagle down there howling and yapping, basically doing about anything he could to coax us into getting him out. The first time my wife went down to get him, she realized that the crate technique didn't stop our little delinquent from spraying graffiti on the walls of his plastic enclosure. This practice continued for days, and as I would lie in bed listening to the muffled complaints of my wife as she cleaned up the puppy during the wee hours of the morning, I couldn't help but wonder if he was worth all the trouble.

The breaking point came at dawn on a Sunday. We decided to tie him up outside so he could fertilize our yard at will, thus ensuring that we could sleep-in without having to worry about his cleanliness. But what we didn't expect is for him to yelp and howl incessantly for us at around 6:00 am. Since he was outside, and since we had our pillows over our heads, the barking was bearable... but apparently not for our neighbor. I can still remember how his tone started out low and forceful but then rose to great, screeching heights, "Shut that dog up (a slight pause for a breath) NOW!!!"

In light of all the evidence urging us to accept that fact that we were puppy-challenged, we decided that Mr. Beagle should have a home out in the country with another family, a family who had cows and chickens and other such animals that would keep Mr. Beagle company when the sun was just beginning to rise. Thus our days of dog ownership came to an abrupt end and remained that way for years, that is, until it seemed good and right in my wife's eyes that our boys have a dog of their own.

She presented the case masterfully, like a skillful orator before a jury, convincing me with indisputable points and utilizing the techniques of logic to anticipate and constrain the doubts that I might be considering. Her most powerful weapon of all was the manipulation of human emotions.

"Shall we deprive our children of sweet memories? Shall they grow up without having the joy of naming their own pet? Did you not have your own dog to hug and play with when you were a lonely, little boy?"

In light of all these arguments, I was forced to say, "I have no objections, your honor."

That's how we ended up with another dog. But even though I loved to see my children rejoice over their new pet, and even though my wife was obviously enjoying the new addition to our home, I didn't have to like Mac as they did. I just had to live with him and exercise a certain congeniality towards the furry critter.

They say that dogs are aware of our feelings, that they even have a sixth sense. I don't know about the latter, but I could see in his eyes that he knew something was askew between us. I don't know if something tipped him off as to my profession, or if he noticed that I would shoot him distrustful looks through squinty eyes, but sometimes he would turn his attention away from the boys and just stare at me- stare a little too long for my liking. There was no doubt that he definitely liked Bek the best, the boys second and me a distant third.

Since Mac was full grown when we got him, he had a hard time adapting to the energy of our boys. You might say that they were just a little too loud for him, a bit too touchy-feely. He put up with their antics, but found solace ultimately in the lap of my wife. She was definitely the only one he really liked.

Without the slightest engineering on my part, there arose a problem with Mac. One day, when I returned home from work, I was greeted by a concerned wife.

"Mac snapped at Calvin twice," she informed, "actually bit him once today. No, he's all right. The bite didn't do much, but I'm a little concerned about Mac's ability to adjust to our kids. I think he may be too old for them."

I rubbed my chin and tried to muster a grave expression all the while secretly delighting in the opportunity that was presenting itself to me. I had to play my cards just right or the whole thing could fall apart.

As I began my speech, I realized that it was suddenly I who had now taken the floor as the prosecutor. I carefully crafted an argument explaining that it was our duty as parents to protect our children from dogs, albeit good dogs, but misunderstood ones, yes, dogs that were meant to lead a quieter life, a better life, really. Surely we as responsible mothers and fathers have an obligation to send off our well-intentioned Mac to a better place. It would be what he would want, after all. That's right. He would step forward, if he could, and implore us to make the right decision. For children and dog, my dear wife. For children and dog...

When I finished my perfumed presentation, I eagerly watched for any signs of agreement. The only reaction was a slight hesitation. But to the experienced eye of this husband that meant seeds of surrender were taking root. With a little more work and a couple disingenuous "It's too bad, isn't it?" we were well on our way to returning Mac to the pound.

And thus it turned out that Mac remained with us for no longer a stint than Mr. Beagle of old. We packed up the gear that we had bought- his crate, his dog bowl, his leash- and returned Mac to the pound. We asked them to find good home for our dog and they assured us that it was likely because of the free doggy gear that would accompany his adoption.

"Anything free is a pretty powerful incentive," they said.

My wife and boys were bummed by the loss of Mac, but they actually took it all quite well. Life went on and soon Mac was forgotten...

Chapter 17

The Regular

"The work week for full-time regulars shall be forty (40) hours per week, eight (8) hours per day within ten (10) consecutive hours..."

-The National Agreement, article 8, section 1-

"The above shall not apply to part-time employees..."

-The National Agreement, article 8, section 3-

"Good morning, Victim."

"Hey, Travis."

And then, while Travis was walking away, he would say, "Poor, poor, Victim."

When I took over City 15 as the new regular, Travis took great pleasure in greeting me this way. And he did this pretty much every day, for I was a victim in his eyes, not a genuine victim, the kind one pities and provides comfort for, but rather someone whom he could greet with a great deal of ironic pleasure. This was because Travis used to be the regular carrier on City 15. He had walked its streets for years and was more than qualified to judge whether or not my present circumstances warranted the status of "victim." Now he's a maintenance man, free from the heavy bag and the tumultuous weather, free from the daily pressures of moving the mail out in a timely fashion, and most of all, he's free from City 15, a route most consider long and arduous, slummy and probably diseased.

Even now, carriers run from City 15, actually flee in terror. When a substitute sees this route number next to their name on the schedule, they begin to weep and beg management for mercy. Without a doubt, it's one the worst routes in the entire office. And in the early summer of 2000, it belonged to me. I was its new regular. But as I stood in the case of City 15 surveying the 647 potential deliveries, I felt thankful. I had endured the hardships of being a PTF for nearly five long years, and I was more than ready to escape the tortures of that position.

Yes, the poor PTF.

All new carriers, no matter their intelligence, no matter their size or physical prowess, or their butt kissing abilities, start out as a mere PTF, which stands for "Part-Time Flexible," denoting two important truths. One, they are flexible, which means that they are floaters; substitutes who fill in wherever there is need. They aren't assigned one route, but all the routes, or more accurately, the crappier routes. Two, they are said to be "Part-Time," which is terribly misleading since they typically work well past the forty hour mark each week (usually six days a week and up to ten hours a day, carrying extra well beyond what one route affords).

These new carriers are first sent off to a weeklong training session where they learn how to case up mail, drive on the passenger side, and follow postal regulations. The schooling moves forward at an easy pace and is usually filled with much donut eating while watching videos and listening to the instructor tell stories. It's an enjoyable time and fills the PTF's mind with grand notions. But it's short lived. For when he arrives at work, smiling and eager to deploy his newly learned skills, he quickly discovers that he's essentially nothing more than a whipping boy, a creature designed only to fulfill his supervisor's every whim.

"Here you go," announces the supervisor, "carry this route and a few relays for Stan. He's got a doctor's appointment today. So grab the extra on your way out. Yeah, that pile over there. No, the big one. Yup, that's it. Here's a map. Be back before dark."

Now if you're Stan, the carrier leaving early for a doctor's appointment, are you going to give away your crème-de-la-crème relays or the monster ones that weigh a hundred-and-forty pounds, are inhabited by thousands of roaming dogs and go uphill both ways? And thus the PTF picks up the extra relays, sets them on a cart, along with his assigned route, which is overloaded and heaping with parcels, and heads out to the dock where he tries to organize the precarious pile of trays and boxes in the back of his truck in a neat and orderly manner, which isn't possible, because it requires a working knowledge of the route.

While on the dock, casually smoking a cigarette, one of the managers adds a word of encouragement, a word which all mailmen everywhere and for all time have heard with great assurance, "Just follow the mail, and you'll be fine."

Just follow the mail.

It's as simple as that. Look at the letter, read the address, look at the house, read the number and proudly drop the letter into the receptacle. Repeat this process and voila! The route is done. It's that simple.

And yet, for all its simplicity, the poor PTF languishes, spinning and turning here and there, squinting at houses, trying desperately and hopelessly to accomplish those final two steps, namely, reading the number on the house and proudly dropping the letter into the receptacle. This, of course, is because many, many houses, houses of all shapes and sizes and worth, yes, everything from tiny trailers to brick mansions, even castles and skyscrapers, don't feel it is necessary to advertise their street addresses. And this greatly troubles the PTF who cannot hope to know whether the yellow two story house in the middle of the block is 1422 George or whether it's the white house next to it, because neither have a discernable street number.

So when this happens, what shall he do? Bundle up the mail and bring it back? Not a good idea. Knock on the door and ask? Certainly not. He's under a time crunch. It takes far too long to do that. So then what? Guess? Yes, more often than not, the PTF resorts to simple guesswork, blindly dropping off the mail, hoping with all his heart that it's the correct address.

But even here there is a problem. For proudly placing the letter into the mailbox requires knowing one bit of crucial information: where the mailbox is in fact located. And while many hang their mailboxes in plain sight, usually next to the front door, there are a vast collection of others far less noticeable, indeed, perfectly camouflaged. Sometimes an overgrown bush is hiding it. Sometimes it's around back. Or it's posted on the side. Or maybe it's this wooden crate on the ground near the front door? Or maybe there's a door slot? But a door slot where? Cut into the side of the house? Around back? Behind the front storm door? And on it goes, ad infinitum.

Over the course of my career, I have seen just about every imaginable mailbox location. And there have been some so wildly hidden, so fantastically concealed, requiring special instructions from the owner, that one can't help but wonder why anyone in their right mind would place the receptacle there. One house in particular comes to mind. It had a secret compartment built into the wall near the front door. To the naked eye, it was nearly invisible, except for maybe the faint outline of a very thin line, square in shape. When pressed correctly, a tap on the upper right hand corner, a panel would unlatch, revealing an inner compartment, and there, leaning upright, an outgoing letter.

For the PTF, all this is maddening; wandering around properties, walking aimlessly through the twisting corridors of corporate buildings, entering backyards only to be attacked by dogs, hearing the continual tick tock of the clock in his ear, thereby causing him to feel more and more desperate as time slips away and the sun sets, spelling failure. Some outright quit. And most, at some point or another, break down in tears. It's the pressure of making it back combined with the utter frustration of it all. The two mixed together form a potent brew.

Because of this, carriers like to bet how long new PTFs are going to last.

A red-head walks in. A new PTF. She's short, petite and in her late-twenties. The regulars watch and rub their chins in contemplation. And then at lunch, while gathered around a table at Fazoli's, the predictions come in.

"Two weeks. I give her two weeks."

"Ah, come on. It's spring. I give her until August."

"August? Too long. I say six weeks tops. Did you look at her build? She's tiny!"

"Well, whatever," says another, "I'm going bold. I'm saying two days."

Laughter.

"Two days?"

"Laugh all you want, but they're sending her out on City five."

"City five?"

"Yup."

Loud groaning.

"City five, huh?"

And on it goes until most everyone settles on a timeframe.

The general consensus for me was two weeks. And when I made it past the two week mark, they all swore that I wouldn't make it out of January. But I did. Barely.

The PTF is a man without a home. A ship without an anchor. For just about the time he becomes proficient at one route, he gets jostled over to another, forced to start from scratch again. This means thousands of new names, new cases, new dogs, new secrets, new streets, new everything. And besides being hunted down on those rare occasions when he's scheduled off, the PTF also has to be weary of early morning calls from management concerning a new starting time.

Let's say that PTF is scheduled to work at 7:00 am. Sometime around 5:20 am, he receives a wake-up call from the boss.

"Hey, good morning. Look, I need you to come in a little earlier today. Plan on coming in at 6:30, alright? Ok, great. I'll see you then. Buh-bye."

Somebody called in sick, and so they need the PTF to case up the vacant route, pie it out to the other carriers and then case up a route of his own, carry it, along with some extra.

This is the PTF's life, and it stinks.

PTFs, therefore, see themselves as objects of pity, sojourners making their way through the wilderness towards the Promised Land, that land flowing with milk and honey, that place which offers hope and rest to weary souls. You see, the land of the Regular provides a mailman with a set day off in addition to Sunday. But there's more. Regulars only have to work overtime if they want it. That just might be the grandest blessing. If a Regular so chooses, he can bathe in the warm waters of the forty-hour work week, handing off relays left and right to some new group of lamentable PTFs. It's truly glorious.

And so on the PTF presses, working and waiting, looking ahead to that time when someone either quits, retires or, yes, dare I say it, dies, so that when a route opens up, he'll become crowned with that ineffable position, the Regular... but only if he's the PTF with the highest seniority. This explains why it can take years before a substitute is in a position to cross over into the Promised Land. Patience and endurance, these are the key ingredients, if he's going to make it to the finish line. A lot of patience, and endurance, and a medicine cabinet stocked with a variety of pain killers, anti-depressants and antacids.

While I was a PTF, my family often talked about the party they were going to throw when I finally made Regular, how we were going eat big, fat, juicy steaks and celebrate the occasion with shouts of acclamation and joy. By the way we talked, one might have supposed we were going to fire Ak47s into the air while yelling, in that Middle Eastern kind of way, "Lalalalalalalala."

During that time of watching and waiting, my mom often inquired into the health of the older carriers asking, "Those fat ones can't live forever, can they? How do they seem?" It's true, there are some beefy carriers, some real gut busters, but their tickers are strong and steady. I suppose it's a testimony to just how healthy walking really is.

So as I was saying, I would often dream of working only five days a week and salivate at the prospect of working eight hours a day. But there was more. My wife was expecting our first child and I wanted consistency when the little guy came along. I wanted more predictability to my schedule as well as fewer hours. And so my wife prayed. She prayed that I would become a Regular by the time the baby was born.

I can still remember the look on the supervisor's face when he came out on the route to tell me that I needed to see my wife. His eyes were wide, voice full of urgency, "Brownie, you're wife called from the doctor's office. You need to get over there now! Don't worry about anything else, just go!" Boy, did I go. About 43.2 seconds later I skidded into the doctor's office and received news that my wife was in the beginning stages of labor. It was four weeks before her due date, but that apparently didn't mean a whole lot to our baby. He was ready to come out.

It's a good thing I hurried, because about eighteen hours later the doctor wrestled him out.

The Family Leave Act permits fathers to take some time off for a new baby. Two weeks seemed good to me. When I entered those two weeks, I was still a PTF. When I returned to work, I learned that I would be the new Regular on City 15. God graciously answered our prayers. And so within the span of about a month, I was rejoicing, not only over a healthy baby boy, but also over finally becoming a Regular. It was an amazing time.

The party we threw wasn't exactly wild and crazy. Calvin was a colicky baby, so that, in addition to our inexperience as parents, had a way of knocking the party out of us. I can vaguely remember a store bought cake, a few balloons taped to my parent's ceiling and a celebration that proved to be anything but rowdy. Everyone was too tired for that, and Ak47s would definitely wake the baby.

But it was all good. City 15, with all its white trash splendor, with all its backbreaking promise, with all of its strange inhabitants, was mine, every last mile of it.

Chapter 18

ᴀ Regular Walk

"When sometimes I am reminded that the mechanics and shopkeepers stay in their shops not only all the forenoon, but all the afternoon too, sitting with crossed legs, so many of them~as if the legs were made to sit upon, and not to stand or walk upon~I think that they deserve some credit for not having all committed suicide long ago."

-Henry David Thoreau-

If you had to guess how many steps you take in a day, what would you say? 6000? 30,000? 150,000? Well, if you're an average American, you take somewhere between 3,000 to 5,000 steps each day. Is that good? If you're missing a leg, it's not bad at all. But if not, then you would be described as having a sedentary lifestyle. If you pushed the average up to 10,000 steps, which is what the fitness gurus recommend, then you're beginning to have what is called an active life, walking roughly 5 ½ miles each day. But since we live in such an affluent society, 10,000 steps is often a difficult figure to achieve. We sit behind desks all day, stare endlessly at computers, spend the evening in front of a TV, microwave our food, order carry-out, drive everywhere and take the elevator.

Amish communities, on the other hand, because they operate without many of these modern conveniences, live radically differently, and it shows in their health. One study looked at 98 Amish adults and found that men, on average, took over 18,000 steps per day. The women took over 14,000 steps. Not bad, eh? Compare that with Joe Technology's 5,000 step average, and it's easy to see why 31% of the general American public is bursting at the seams, while only about 4% of the Amish are obese.

Since our lives are full of so many exercise-free conveniences, we have to look for ways to fill the gap. And so we manufacture walking. We purchase machines with moving treads, jump on contraptions that simulate climbing stairs, or pay a monthly fee so that we can walk next to a bunch of sweaty strangers while staring at a mounted flat screen. In some respects it's strange, or at least historically peculiar, but for most people that's what has to be done if they're going to stay fit.

Things are different for the mailman. About the last thing you'll see a letter carrier on is a treadmill, unless of course they're anorexic. There are those. But most mailmen get all the walking they could ever want from nine-to-five.

I'm often asked how far I walk each day, and for the longest time I didn't know. I would usually answer the question with a shrug, and say, "More than I want." Curiosity finally got the best of me, so I purchased one of those nifty, little pedometers, calibrated it, tested it to make sure it was working properly and then set out on a normal day's walk. When I finished the route, I looked down and saw a surprising figure. I had taken over 22,000 steps. That's around eleven miles! And it's not eleven miles of whistle a tune, flat, care-free walking either. We climb countless stairs, sometimes eleven or twelve leg-burning, heart-pumping steps to reach one house. Then there's also the mailbag. While packed full of magazines and thick catalogs, maybe a parcel or two and a bundle of letters, it's as if we're walking with a right hip in its third trimester.

It's no wonder then that mailmen often complain of aching knees or ailing backs. Most end up having surgery at some point too. But nearly all have exceedingly strong legs and wildly firm buns. That's a perk, I suppose.

Regarding the routes themselves, the most significant fact is this: not all routes are created equal. This is to say that not all of the routes in an office are going to bless you with a highly active life. Some have portions of curbside delivery, or what might also be called driving relays. And some consist entirely of driving relays, which are called mounted routes. These are the crème de la crème routes, the granddaddies of all postal desire. Carriers clamor for these routes. Yearn for them. Fight for them.

Deep down inside, right at the core of their beings, mailmen long to join the ranks of the sedentary. They want to expend all their energy pushing a gas pedal and replace their heavy bag with a seatbelt. They want to trade in their sore feet for a cushioned seat and remain stationary for hours on end, turning only slightly to their left and then to the right, back to the left for more letters and then back to the right, depositing the mail into a box seven inches from the window. But only those with the most seniority can hope to attain this blessed state. That's how our system works. If you've put in enough time, you're awarded a good route. If you haven't put in enough time, you're awarded buns of steel. So not all mailmen walk eleven miles every day. But many do.

Strangely enough, even with all their aches and pains, there's still something deeply alluring about walking for the mailman. It's as if there's an inner craving to walk, a desire within our legs to stretch out, to feel the earth under our feet. It's hard to explain, but after doing the same thing for so long, it's like the human body grows accustomed to the act and programs into its system a sense of satisfaction, or a sense of feeling at home, when the action is performed. The first few steps on a crisp morning bring with them pleasure, feelings of contentment, something not unlike a runner's high. The problem is how quickly it goes away. By about the third mile, we're once again dreaming of those carriers driving the mail, and how good the sensation of slowly becoming fat must feel for them at that very moment.

What possesses someone when they're walking through the lawn and garden section at a local home improvement store, to say, "Look, Harry! Look at those plastic deer over there in the corner. Those would be perfect in our front lawn." For the life of me, I can't understand the appeal of lawn ornaments. But people buy them. They buy a lot of them. In the course of my daily rounds, I'll walk by dancing frogs waving hello (or maybe goodbye, I'm not sure which), flocks of plastic geese, smiling ducks, flaming flamingos, scowling gargoyles, roosters, strange looking cupids and lighthouses of all shapes and sizes. Some position a statue of St. Francis right in the middle of their garden, while others prefer the image of a large gardener bending over, a hint of butt crack proudly on display. There are also those shiny glass balls on pedestals. Why someone would put a reflective, red ball in the center of their lawn is beyond me. But people do it. And apparently like it.

As a regular, the scenery never changes. On an intellectual level I knew this would be true, but until I had experienced the reality first hand, and for an extended period of time, I couldn't really comprehend what it meant. It means that you walk by the same houses, listen to the same barking dogs, stroll under the same trees, trod over the same cracked sidewalks, step over the same toys and, yes, admire the same cheesy lawn ornaments day after day. In contrast to the PTF's life, which is ever changing and unpredictable, the regular's life is saturated with the familiar and characterized by repetition. One might say it's robotic. And because of this, it's easy to drift off to faraway places, to dream dreamy things and forget about your surroundings. That's another thing about walking. It seems to stimulate deep thinking and stir the imagination. Sometimes a long drive will produce the same hypnotic effect, but for me, it's almost exclusive to walking the mail. While lost in one of these dreamy states, I'm convinced that I've written great speeches or composed moving melodies, even penetrated the depths of certain philosophical quandaries. But as is so often the case, just as I'm digging deeper and deeper into the mines of unearthed reflections, quarrying out valuable nuggets of insight, the ingenious thought wavers and then suddenly disappears. I'll joyously scribble down my idea on a scrap piece of paper only to later find the truncated saying either undecipherable or entirely unextraordinary outside of its once fertile context.

Frederick Nietzsche was right when he said, "All truly great thoughts are conceived by walking.[3]" Though he needed to add, "But are hopelessly lost while delivering the mail."

At other times, possibly after having watched a show recounting the story of several mangled shipmates trying to survive on a deserted island, I'll imagine what I might have done in a similar situation. What would I use to bandage up my wounded companions? Would I be able to smack a dislocated shoulder back into place? Should you char a bloody stump shut? What about food? Does eating a crab raw make one sick? Or what if one of my

---

[3] Just to be clear, that's about the only thing Nietzsche and I would agree on.

shipmates dies? Is it morally wrong to eat another human being? Would I want someone nibbling on my femur?

When I stir and realize that I've been moving along like an automaton, completely unaware of my surroundings, the wonder of people receiving their neighbor's mail suddenly becomes the subject of new, more unpleasant imaginations. When I get back to the office, I'm greeted by a number of yellow sticky notes on my case telling me about irate customers who called in complaining. One might read, "Mrs. Thompson called. She was very angry. Received neighbor's mail. I don't want to have to talk to her again. So watch your delivery!"

It's not like putting the right name in the right box is difficult- a monkey with good knees could do it- but there's something about walking, in combination with the fresh air and the hundreds and hundreds of addresses that pass before your eyes that make daydreaming irresistibly alluring.

There's definitely a negative side to being left alone with one's own thoughts for hours on end. It's called worrying. It may sound silly, but I've actually been tempted to call home to my wife and ask her to keep a close watch on the boys while they eat their chicken nuggets for lunch. In case they need the Heimlich maneuver performed, I want her to be close at hand. Or maybe I'll start thinking about my basement and how toxic molds are almost certainly the cause of some recent flu-like symptoms. Once these ideas get inside your head, almost no amount of mental bucking can knock the unlikely scenario off the brain.

But there are also those more realistic problems that can dominate a person's thoughts. It might be financial troubles or health problems, possibly wayward children or aging parents. These are some of the things that can really steal your peace. I know a number of carriers who have almost gone mad while brooding over such problems while out on the route. Facing marital problems, they mull over past fights or stressful conversations, replaying arguments over and over again in their minds. When they come strolling back into the office, the toll of anxiety is evident on their faces. They've obviously been thinking about their problems all day. Sometimes they need counseling or meds. And sometimes when we're made aware of these situations, the occasional conversation about how likely they are of going postal transpires.

While dipping a fry into his ketchup, one carrier asks, "You think Perry could go postal?"

One responds, "You know, I could definitely see him snapping."

"No, no, he's not going to go postal." retorts a female carrier. "Besides, he hardly seems like the gun type. I doubt he's ever even owned a BB gun."

While chewing on a fry, "Yeah, maybe. Well I suppose it's the quiet ones that you have to watch out for anyway- bottling it up and all, never lettin' off any steam."

"Now, Hartman," begins the female carrier, "I could definitely see him losing it."

The others nod thoughtfully as they contemplate the name. After a moment's reflection and a few more nods, somebody suddenly asks, "You didn't see that Cubs game yesterday, did ya? Another heartbreak loss..."

When Letter Carrier Rodger Parker looked in his rearview mirror, he saw something that would profoundly alter his appointed rounds that day. He saw a truck driving on a sidewalk, careening, running over small pines, rapidly approaching a large lake.

While returning home from the hospital, Robert and Betty Byington's brakes had suddenly failed as they approached a red light. Not wanting to slam into the cars in front of him, Robert swerved off the road. Moments later he was down an embankment, skipping across water, sinking quickly.

Parker, a twelve year Navy veteran, immediately responded, diving into the water, swimming out to rescue the Byington's.

"I rolled down my window and there was Mr. Parker, just in that instant," said Betty, recounting the story.

Parker grabbed a hold of the woman and quickly pulled her out the window. By now two other people were trying to free Robert from the sinking vehicle but were having difficulty. When Parker turned his attention to Robert, water was swirling around his neck.

"I just grabbed him and kind of jerked him three or four times until I could get him out of the vehicle before it completely submerged underwater," Parker recalled.

When Robert and Betty were both safely ashore, Parker left, wanting to remain anonymous. But he didn't remain anonymous for long. When the Postmaster assembled the carriers together the next day, requesting that the rescuer step forward, only then did Parker admit to his having saved the Byington's. Parker was soon recognized as The National Association of Letter Carriers Hero of the Year for 2003.

Betty later said, "God is all great, greater than any of us. But the greatest angels on earth are the heroes. And, Mr. Parker is a hero."

Once in a while a mailman's regular rounds are interrupted by the sight or sounds of distress. It's true that no one in my office has ever pulled someone out of a sinking truck, but there have been those who have gone the extra mile to help their patrons. One of my fellow carriers, a guy by the name of Philman, once inclined his ear to what sounded like someone calling out for help. Wandering around, trying to figure out where the voice was coming from, he finally pinpointed the source. It was coming from inside a nearby house. Knocking on the door, he heard a desperate cry, "Help, I'm stuck in the bathroom. Come in and help me!" Entering and weaving his way through the house, he found himself confronted with a large woman stuck in a bathtub. Grabbing where he could and struggling with all his might, he finally dislodged the slippery woman from her watery prison. He was called a hero. We just wanted to know if she gave him a hug after being rescued.

I heard about another heroic act first hand from an old man on City 3. When I drove up to his mailbox, he stood leaning on his cane, looking to chat. Since I wasn't the regular on his route, he asked where Lonnie was. When I told him that he was on vacation, he said, "Yeah, that Lonnie, he's a good guy. I like him. You know I was working out in the yard one day and fell over- couldn't get off my ass to save my life. I was just sitting there stuck. About that time, here comes Lonnie up the street, driving by. I start waving my arms for help, but he just waves back and keeps on going. I'm thinking, 'What the hell, he just left me here.' Well here he comes around again, asking if I needed something, and I says, "Well, hell yeah, I need something. I'm down here and can't get up.' So he comes over, puts his arms under mine, right here, and man, he lifted me right up, no problem. That Lonnie, he's strong."

My own acts of heroism have been far more modest. I once tried to open a frozen car door for an elderly woman, but failed miserably, so that hardly counts. I may have broken the handle in the struggle.

About the only other story worthy of mention is when I happened upon an elderly woman in a wheelchair calling out, "Bun! Bun, where are you?" The woman looked and sounded distressed.

While approaching, I asked, "Is everything all right?"

Her back was facing me, so when she tried to turn her wheelchair around, using only her pink slippered feet to perform the action, she began to roll backwards, due to a slight decline in the sidewalk.

"Help! Ahhh, catch me!" She cried.

She clearly wasn't in any real danger, so I didn't need to dive in the path of her wheelchair in order to stop her from flying out into the street or off a cliff. The cracks in the sidewalk were enough to bring her to a quick stop. Regardless, one thing was clear, she didn't have any business wandering around outside by herself.

"What are you doing out here?" I asked. At that moment, I noticed that she had one of those help buttons dangling from her neck, the "I've fallen and can't get up" types.

She moaned, "My doggie has run away. I can't find my doggie."

"Okay, well we'll look for your dog, but let's first get you back inside. Where do you live? Down there? The gray house on the corner? Alright, let me push you back."

Her home was just down the street, a small, somewhat moldy, plain building surrounded by a chain-link fence. When we arrived at the gate leading to her backyard, I stared down at one, six-inch high step. Following the cement path with my eyes, I could see that there were four more steps leading up to her backdoor.

I pondered the situation.

"You can call me Twinkie." She announced, staring up at me.

"Oh, okay. Hi, Twinkie. Hey, uh, how are we supposed to get you up all these stairs?"

She suddenly leaned forward. While holding onto the fence, grunting and straining, joints popping, she began to pull herself up.

"Here, help me up." She grunted.

I puzzled over how to help. I mean, where does one grab exactly? It's not as if there were handles on her. And she also had a lot of rounded corners, if you know what I mean.

My first instinct was to stand beside her and kind of gingerly pull up on one arm, to go with the usher technique. But she needed more than that. A lot more. It quickly became apparent that I needed to really get in there and snuggle up, to grab and grip and engage in some serious tugging, if I was going to get the job done. So that's what I did. I moved in, imitating to the best of my ability the Postmaster's technique for proper lifting.

Once she was up and stable and catching her breath, we eyed the six inch step before us. One might have thought we were looking at Mount Kilimanjaro.

You know how a gymnast, after performing a quadruple back, no-look, twisting gainer, looks when they try to stick their landing, how their body quivers as each muscle strains to remain stationary, how their faces are marked with concentration and pain, and how their arms extend out, fingers flexed, feeling for balance? Well, that's how Twinkie looked when she thrust her foot forward, successfully planting it atop the step. She stuck the landing. But only partially. The other foot still remained miles away from reaching the summit. And so there she stood, half leaning, more like hunching, frozen and perplexed with one foot up, the other down. Without help, I think she would have remained fixed in that position for days, maybe even weeks.

After successfully negotiating the first hurdle, we arrived at the four steps leading up to her back door.

I can't honestly say I remember a whole lot about our ascent. I think I've repressed those memories. But I do remember wishing I had a pulley. And I do remember a moment near the end, as she stood poised on the uppermost step, when my life flashed before my eyes. While trying to lunge into a wheelchair positioned in front of her, she swayed dangerously in all directions, teetering here and there like a tree about to topple. Had she fallen backwards, I would still be on her steps, a strangely reddish blue stain.

Once safely inside, firmly planted in her wheelchair, she said, "Oh, thank you, mailman. Thank you. Now could you look for my doggie? Would you look for him outside?" I agreed and went outside, calling, "Bun! Here, boy (whistle, whistle). Bun!"

Standing on a sidewalk yelling "Bun" isn't exactly considered normal behavior, so I sheepishly shouted the dog's name a few more times and then hurried back inside. Twinkie repositioned herself in the kitchen.

Walking in, I said, "Sorry, I didn't see him."

The elderly woman covered her face, "Oh, where did he go? Where did my doggie go? If something happened to my doggie..."

As I moved forward to comfort her, she looked up and said, "mailman, would you do me a favor? Look around and see if he's in here. Look on my bed. He likes my bed." She pointed toward her bedroom.

After walking down a narrow hallway, I entered her bedroom. Clothes and food wrappers were flung everywhere, and an unpleasant smell hung in the air. Her bed was extremely messy too. Cream colored blankets piled high formed a kind of mountain range around the spot where she entered and exited the bed.

I glanced about a moment longer and then decided to leave. But that's when I noticed, or at least I thought I noticed, something white in the center of the bed. Moving closer, I considered the object. A twinge of horror shot through me. For there, lying on its side, feet fully extended, was a white, very still, sporadically hairy, pink-skinned dog. My heart sank. It had to be Bun, and he didn't look good at all.

Staring intently at its chest, I held my breath as I watched for signs of life. His side, ever so slightly, *ever so slowly*, lifted, and then ever so slightly lowered.

"Bun? Bun, is that you?" I whispered. I called out again, though this time more loudly.

No movement. Not even a twitch.

Returning to the kitchen, I announced, "Hey, your dog's on your bed, uh, apparently sleeping soundly."

The woman looked thrilled. I felt kind of sick.

"Now listen, Twinkie," I urged her, "you promise me that you won't go outside looking for your dog anymore, okay? You're going to get hurt out there."

She promised, looked around blankly and then asked, "Have you seen my dog? I think he's missing."

"*Huh?*"

"My dog, I don't know where he's at."

Oh, no.

Right then, the back door swung open and a young girl bounded into the room, followed by a middle-aged woman with dark short hair. They were relatives of Twinkie.

"Twinkie," began the woman with a smile, "whatcha up to now? Are you stayin' out of trouble?"

I explained what had happened, ending with, "Bun's in there on her bed." I then made a beeline for the backdoor.

"Well, gotta go. My rounds are calling."

I'm thinking it's probably best if Twinkie forgets about this particular act of postal heroism. And I'm pretty certain she already has.

Chapter 19

Little Beirut

"It was a pretty rough neighborhood where I grew up. The really tough places were over around Third Avenue where it ran into the Harlem River, but we weren't far away."

-Norman Rockwell-

After accounting for vacation days, sick days, holidays and normal days off, I figure that I've walked by each and every house on City 15 approximately 1,123 times, which means, more significantly, that I've had the unique task of venturing into a region affectionately referred to as Little Beirut; ~~a gloriously felonious and downright dangerous, Mos Eisley Cantina~~ an underprivileged and challenged neighborhood spanning an area approximately eight blocks long and at least three blocks wide.

This is the place where children cuss each other out for entertainment, where strange people wander about, where mangy dogs run loose, where houses slump, cars make funny noises, and where a muddy river perfumes the region with some really interesting smells. It's my Midwest ghetto. Only here have I seen cops running down an alley after a fleeing punk, or cops, with their guns drawn, talking a man out of a parked car. But besides the smattering of police activity, there are also a lot of people out and about. Some of this is due to the fact that Little Beirut is located towards the end of my route, which means that the mail is delivered when kids are arriving home from school and when people are returning home from work. There's also a large concentration of the unemployed hanging out here as well. So when you add it all up, Little Beirut is an area teeming with people. It's a grand mixture of the bizarre, the almost normal and the generally mischievous.

But for these very reasons, it's kind of fun to deliver the mail here, because you just don't meet people like this on Sunny-Well-To-Do Lane.

It is, therefore, worth taking a short tour through the neighborhood.

Toward the beginning of the first relay you'll meet a Mr. Walters, a grey-haired man with spunky eyes, an old Harley dude, who always asks, no matter how sunny or cloudy it might be, "You think it's gonna rain?" This man has the unique ability of detecting my presence no matter how sneaky I try to be. Just as I'm about to drop the mail into his box, the door swings open. He's standing there, hand outstretched for the mail, question ready to fire. "Hey, partner! Think it's gonna rain?" From somewhere around his house I can hear a strange, high pitched sound that rises up to a squeal, fades off and then rises to another squeal. It's really annoying. When I finally asked what the sound was, he scrunched his face and said in a serious tone, "Why, you can't hear that. Only dogs can." And then after a moment's reflection, he added, "But it's a kind of siren that keeps the mutts away. They don't like it. But only dogs can hear it, not humans."

On one of the side streets, nestled under a congregation of maples, is Mr. EBay's house. Hardly a day goes by that he doesn't receive a parcel or two, or three, or six. Every route has one of these collector types. These folks gorge themselves with Beanie Babies or coins or whatever else had only fifteen minutes of time remaining before the glittering trinket was no longer available. As for Mr. EBay, he loves glassware. When I knock on his door, he pokes his head out, looks to the left and then to the right in a suspicious manner, almost as if he were looking for spies, and then greets me with an uneasy hello.

"I've got a few packages for ya."

"Oh, good. Bring 'em on in."

And with that, the door swings open revealing a living room cluttered, and I mean cluttered, with dusty books, scattered newspapers and a wild assortment of oddly colored bottles, their various shapes ranging from the supremely ornate to the smoothly simple. It looks like an alchemist's cove or possibly a wizard's lair. The arcane atmosphere is heightened by two other factors: (1) He has bushy white hair. (2) His wife, who also has bushy white hair, walks around with a parakeet on her shoulder. I'm guessing that it's an imp in disguise.

While signing for a package he mutters, "The uglier they are, the more they're worth."

"Excuse me?"

He looks up, "Seriously, more times than not, it's the uglier pieces of glassware that are worth the most money." He finishes signing for the package, looks up again and adds, "Keep your eyes open at garage sales for those."

Seeing how I don't know the first thing about glassware, I'm not going to question him, but I do wonder why a person would willingly decorate their home with deformed-looking cups. It must be a wizard thing.

Speaking of cluttered spaces, Little Beirut has to have one of the most mind-boggling messy homes, at least in terms of its sheer quantity of junk that I've ever seen. Each time I walk by this particular house, I marvel at how their enclosed front porch is literally filled to the brim with everything from lawn gnomes, to records, to bikes without tires, to you name it. Junk is stacked from the floor clear up to the ceiling. And I'm not talking about a loose pile of stuff either. I'm talking jammed tight, a true vision of a demented packrat's ideal. Parked along the street, right out in front of the house, sits a light blue station wagon equally gorged with trash. The owner, a skinny, older man who wears tight, plaid button ups, makes his presence known only very rarely. I'll see him wandering around his unkempt yard eyeing the grass as if he were looking for something. He's quiet, weird and kind of dirty.

Once, when I looked down at a certified letter with his name on it, I realized that my chance to peek inside his home had arrived. Knocking with an extra measure of "oomph," just to make sure he would hear me, I patiently waited for him to open the door. I heard footsteps, saw the handle turn and then, all at once, I was beholding one of the most incredible sights these mailman eyes have ever seen. Standing before me, sandwiched between two great towering walls of trash, stood the old man.

While trying to hide my surprise, I said, "I've got a certified letter for Mr. Stevens."

"That's me."

Just as I was starting to reach for my pen, he quickly added, "I'll get a pen. Follow me."

Follow me? Follow him where? I thought. As I watched with a mix of eagerness and dread, he turned and began walking down a dimly lit tunnel. Wondering if I would ever return, I reluctantly followed.

Following him, my thoughts were taken back to when I hiked through the Narrows at Zion National Park. There you follow a stream through a tight, curving canyon with smooth walls rising to dizzying heights. In this home there was junk stacked up to the ceiling, without so much as a finger's width to spare, with a three-foot wide path slicing its way through an otherwise stuffed room. I couldn't believe what I was seeing. Nor smelling.

After a short trek, the path I was squeezing my way through widened into a small chamber, a space just large enough for a stained chair, a skinny lamp and a console TV. While the old man was bent over, occupied with signing his name, the lone lamp cast an eerie glow throughout the room. As I stood there surveying my gloomy surroundings, I wondered how many furry critters were watching me from dark crevices.

It's hard to say what all Mr. Stevens had stacked up in the room, but there were vast amounts of old clothes dangling from cardboard clefts as well as a profuse quantity of papers strewn over almost everything. I think I saw a lamp stand poking out at one spot and possibly a toaster oven near the ceiling. It may have been an old VCR though. Honestly, I didn't look around too much. I just wanted out of there.

Little Beirut certainly isn't known for its hygienic zeal, and as such, most homes leave something to be desired in the sanitation department. It's for this reason (and this is my own observation that's certainly open to criticism) that many of the people in poorer neighborhoods often hang outside for long periods of time. I'm guessing they prefer fresh air to the smell of a stale apartment. So as I walk from house to house, I have to dodge kids, slip between people lounging on front steps, and offer up obligatory head nods to shirtless guys milling about the street. Everyone's out. Only the infirmed and drug dealers remain inside.

Smaller children are often afforded great freedom. They wander around with sticks, zip here and there on their trikes, play chicken with moving cars, and are continually being yelled at by their mothers, "Dammit, David, I told you to get out of there! Stop hitting your sister! Come here! Don't! Stop it! David!" After about the four-hundredth, no five-hundredth command, a perturbed father bursts out the front door yelling, "What the hell's going on out there? David, get in here! What do you think you're doing driving us all nuts?"

Elementary-aged children often gather to play ball and can be heard arguing over batting order for twenty minutes. Once that's resolved, a questionable ruling will effectively propel both teams into a state of prepubescent hysteria, thus insuring another twenty minutes of impassioned debate. If they aren't playing ball then they're probably flipping off older kids, smoking, or flirting with an ER visit by performing dangerous tricks while ramping off some homemade, nail infested, "Hey, let's use this pipe" ramp.

Most of the teenagers in Little Beirut prefer the indoors and probably spend most of their time talking on the phone, sitting in front of a computer, or procreating. Once in a while the basketball courts will come alive as girls watch skinny boys fight for rebounds. But by far the most common sight would have to be clingy lovers. While sitting on porches or leaning against cars, skanky couples slobber all over each other, holding one another in a prolonged state of obscene hugging. In time I'll see one of these girls crying something awful with her friends, declaring the world to be unfair and her ex-boyfriend a worthless piece of human excrement. But as she's being consoled, I'll think to myself, *Oh, don't you worry honey, you'll be holding hands with some horney loser before you know it.* And sure enough, in about four weeks, I'll see her and Joe sitting on some porch, locked together in an eternal embrace of lascivious passion, feeling twice the joy as ever before.

Many of the adults live a life of banal car watching. While stretched out across a ledge in front of their house, they find the rhythmic sound of passing vehicles soothing and gain some measure of triumph from the occasional honk they receive from acquaintances. The pimp-mobile, with its thumping bass and racy lyrics, also provides a great deal of head-turning enjoyment.

There was a time when everyone had front porches, an era when people really did know their neighbors. Families would hang out together and enjoy summer evenings, taking time to recount their daily affairs, while swinging back and forth on a wooden swing. But it seems as if the front porch has become a dinosaur, an antiquated concept relegated to the older ways of bygone generations. Newer homes with their air conditioning and attached, two car garages make it possible for people to go days without really seeing their neighbors. We rarely congregate by the swing and eat ice cream together, and almost never exist as a family apart from the mesmerizing glow of the TV. Instead, the newer generation only goes outside to mow, jog or watch their children's endless round of scheduled activities. I can't help but think that something has been lost, that the front porch is intrinsically refreshing. It just seems like people open up to one another there; that life has a way of slowing down. And in this respect, neighborhoods like Little Beirut have it right. They still understand what it means to be a community, even if the scenes played out in their neck of the woods fall something short of a Norman Rockwell painting.

My own role in Little Beirut varies greatly from house to house. Some people like to chat while others hardly take notice of my presence, but amid this spectrum there's definitely one constant. Low income areas have a notoriously high moving rate, and as such, I'm constantly trying to figure out who's living at each residence. It isn't uncommon, therefore, to see a wrinkled letter sticking out of a mailbox with the following inscription scribbled across the front, "Don't Live Here!" This is their way of letting us know that the particular addressee has moved out. But just in case you didn't notice, the statement "Don't Live Here" is simply a command to avoid taking up residency at the place. So, as I trust you can imagine, I've been more than a little tempted to write, "Don't worry. I wasn't planning on it," and put it back in their box. But I refrain. Instead, I drop off a change of address form and figure there's about a 25% chance of completion. About the only way to get to the bottom of things is to ask people directly.

I'll say, "So, uh, who's living here these days?"

"Collins and Monika Timmons."

"Ok, thanks."

"Oh, wait, Amanda Collins is gone. Don't leave her mail here... And if you get mail for Bruce or Mary Eldridge, that's good. Well, and you might also get mail with my maiden name on it- Harlow, look for Harlow. "

"Is that all?"

"I think so."

While we mailmen try to keep up with the ever changing roster of low income neighborhoods, another kind of confusion is introduced by these three simple words: Or Current Resident. Hispanics sometimes don't understand what it means and often think it's somebody else's name, a Mr. O.C. Resident, apparently. Confident that it doesn't belong to them, they circle the phrase, write "He no live here" across the front and leave it in the box for me to take back. I come along, shake my head, write "No, this is you," draw an arrow back to the phrase and re-deliver it. This process can continue on for days, as each of us scribble new markings all over the letter in a kind of obstinate, inky duel. The patron usually wins, because he chooses to move away.

Others who are more proficient with English get hung up on the wrong name sitting above the qualifying statement "Or Current Resident." To illustrate, consider the following:

John Doe,
Or Current Resident
1111 East Main Street.
Small Town, USA.

When I'm about two houses away, I hear someone calling out, "Mailman! Mailman! This isn't mine." Looking back, I see some guy waving a letter in the air with an inconvenienced and annoyed expression. While shooting me a look that suggests I'm a moron, he points at the name John Doe and declares, "This guy hasn't lived here for months." In response, I offer him a look that says something like, "I'll see your moron and raise you an illiterate," and then point my finger at the golden statement "Or Current Resident." Sometimes I still have to explain what it means.

I began this chapter by drawing an analogy between Little Beirut and an overweight man's gut. The idea was to focus your attention on one of the more aesthetically challenged regions of City 15. And while it's true that the area has a distinctively Mad Max feel to it, I would be remiss if I didn't talk about one glaring exception. And for that, I'm going to have to introduce you to the Caroways.

Chapter 20

A Perfect Lawn With Two Distinct Blemishes

"Every blade of grass has its Angel that bends over it
and whispers, 'grow, grow.'"

-Talmud-

"Mrs. Joe was a very clean housekeeper, but had an exquisite art of
making her cleanliness more uncomfortable and unacceptable than
dirt itself."

-Charles Dickens, Great Expectations-

———————————

On a green lawn located somewhere in the heart of Little
Beirut, two unusual gardeners tend their lush oasis. With scissors
in hand, two women can be seen crawling around their yard
fastidiously clipping away at each and every naughty blade of grass
daring to grow a millimeter beyond its allotted height.

This is the residence of June and Sally Caroway, a mother
and daughter of considerable age who happen to believe with all
their heart that proper lawn care is the single most important
challenge facing humanity today. And by thus arming themselves
with knee pads and low brimmed hats, lawn bags and garden tools,
these two women attempt to fulfill their botanical vision by
maintaining one of the most immaculate yards conceivable to the
human mind. It doesn't matter if it's the mulch or the edging or
the finely trimmed hedges, every square inch of their lawn glimmers
with the radiant glow of green perfection.

And oh, what beautiful grass they have. It's like a vast army
of dignified soldiers, each blade standing at full attention.

"Chins up, you pointy heads!"

"Sir, yes, sir!"

"The Generals should be waking up soon and I-BRADLEY!!! Quit slouching over there!"

"Sir, I'm sorry, sir!"

"You want to be plucked up, boy?"

"No sir, I don't, sir!"

"You remember what happened to Walters when he leaned a little too much to the right?"

"Unfortunately, I do, sir!"

"Well, then you better get your act together, soldier. We got a caravan of fertilizer coming through today and..."

As I was saying, their grass is truly amazing. But amid all the pristine vegetation, the Caroways are often unhappy, for not everyone in Little Beirut shares their utopian vision of a well-groomed lawn. Actually, nobody does. And this, let me assure you, disturbs our two ladies to no definite end.

Rising from the ground to greet me, the daughter, a slightly overweight woman with thick glasses and rosy cheeks, calls out, "Hey, buddy! How you doin'?"

"Not bad. And you?"

Sally shuffles over and leans in close. The movement resembles that of someone wishing to pass a secret. "I'll tell ya, buddy," she pauses, looks around at some of the neighboring houses, and then continues, "I'd be a lot better if some of these people would just pick up after themselves."

"Oh, yeah?"

"You know how many cigarette butts I've picked up today?"

I shrug.

"Tons of 'em!" A trash bag located in her left hand provides more than enough evidence to substantiate the claim.

You may be wondering how so many cigarette butts end up in their yard given the quality of their care, and so it should be pointed out that she isn't referring to her own property. No, no, she's referring to the neighborhood as a whole. That's right. She and her mother are the keepers of all cleanliness, even if it's a gutter 300 feet away from the edge of their property. And so I'll see them wandering about the neighborhood, bending over and grabbing junk, snatching up wrappers or abandoned fast food bags within about a two or three block radius of their home. At some point they even meander on over to a nearby supermarket parking lot and work that place over too. I have no idea what possesses them to do it, but there they'll be, garbage bag in hand, cleaning up the place as if they were one of the employees. I once asked a kid who worked there, one of those guys who pushes shopping carts back inside, what he thought of the two older women. He was too polite to swirl a finger next to his head, so he chose instead to shrug his shoulders while cracking a firm grin. Whatever it is about the supermarket parking lot in particular, this much is clear, these two women have an insatiable desire to pick up every scrap of paper that can be spied out with their eagle eyes. And by the look on their faces, they love every moment of it.

June, a skinny little thing with a small, wrinkly face, is usually quick to join the conversation. Once she realizes that the subject of our discussion is cleanliness, her eyes sparkle with life, and then, with a voice like that of an old rocking chair, she begins, "Listen, you see them vagabonds over there?"

The old woman points towards a series of homes about half a block away. The houses are a particularly grungy cluster of rentals, large duplexes with busted gutters, chipped paint and a score of other unsightly traits. They're famous for housing riff-raff. Even as she speaks, several tattooed men are milling around the porch, laughing loudly. As one lifts a pop can to his mouth, finishing it off with several large gulps, he then tosses it down on an already littered lawn.

"Why just look at'em. What's wrong with those people?" She begins with a flurry. "Filthy! They're just filthy! You'd think they were animals."

As her mother speaks, the daughter can be seen shaking a disgusted look back and forth with great energy. This in turn energizes June, compelling her to launch some spit towards the apartments. And then, all at once, she curls up her wrinkly hand into a tight fist and declares, "I'd just like to go over there and punch'em in the face."

"Punch'em in the face?" I ask.

"Oh, you betcha. Punch'em right in the face."

Although the sight of June is quite comical, I have absolutely no doubt that she would love nothing more than to go over there and knock one of those guys out. And I think she could.

She continues, "Listen, you know that house just around the corner, the rental over that way?" She points towards the house. "Isn't that just unbelievable? And you know what? I happen to know the woman who owns that place. She lives out in the country on a large plot of land- nice picket fence, shady trees, garden, it's a beautiful home. You oughta see that place. But you know what? She'll let this rental next to us just go to hell- all fallin' in and dumpy. I'd like to ask her, just once, why she's fine with that." She catches her breath and then continues with more volume. "I bet she wouldn't stand for having something like that next to her home. Not a chance! Why, I'd just like to..." and as she winds up for the pitch, another fist appears, "Why I'd just like to punch her in the face too!"

By now it should be plain that June Caroway not only declares Jihad upon all those unclean infidels inhabiting her area, but also upon all those who might aid or abet such people by providing them with shelter.

These two ladies often unload their frustrations, wipe the froth from their mouths and then chat about things like the weather or plants. But there are times when the ranting builds in momentum, opening up new, more extravagant vistas of grumbling.

In a low hush, Sally adds, "Things aren't looking any better either with all the Mexicans running around these days."

Since the opening of a major meat packing plant in our area a decade or more ago, the city of Logansport has seen a major increase in the Latino population. Hispanics are now a common part of our society. And one such family moved in next door to the Caroways, a nice Latino couple with two well-behaved children.

June latches onto the subject and quickly adds, "They oughta stay in their own country and just leave us alone. Can't understand a word they're saying anyway with all their~" At this point it's difficult to describe the sound June makes with her mouth, but while lifting her eyes toward heaven, a noise resembling that of a trilling Indian war cry echoed of out of her.

But as her tongue jumped and jiggled and slithered about like a snake in tall grass, something strange began to happen. A group of tulips next to a small bush started yelling, "You stupid blades of grass, you don't even have a single bloom amongst the whole lot of ya. And what, you think you're going to take over this yard, seeing that you're so numerous and all?" At this, the tulips started whacking the ground with their heads, bending and swatting, crumpling three or four blades of grass with each strike. A number of well-pruned bushes, feeling as though their shapely figures were far more excellent than the ivy growing alongside the house, bristled and started scraping at the vines in an attempt to pull them off the building. Before long the whole garden was in an uproar. The grass was fighting back, slicing away at the stems of the flowers like men with green scimitars. Hydrangeas were launching mulch at pansies and large flocks of annuals were slinging mud at each other. Red geraniums used their fluffy heads to beat against their pink neighbors, and a purple petunia even dared an orange marigold to come over and "say that to his face."

Each plant, as they continued to fight and call each other vile names, felt it was their right to have the property all to themselves. Suddenly a large tree began swaying back and forth. Realizing that he was one of the first to inhabit the yard, as well as feeling generally tired of providing the Caroways with shade, the old tree curled one of its great branchy hands into a tight fist and punched June right in the...

Of course, this part of the story is pure fiction. I mean really, a rose thinking it's superior to a tulip simply because it's a different color, or a tree regarding itself as vegetationally superior just because it inhabited the lawn before the other plants. How ridiculous.

When the Caroways indulged in this kind of blatant bigotry, I would often remind them as gently as I could, and with as many carefully chosen words as I could muster, that they were acting like complete and utter asses.

Such tender rebukes never really affected their racist views, however, so when they worked themselves up into one of these lathers, I would simply hand them their mail and promptly leave.

And so the mailman often continued on his way, leaving behind him, somewhere in the heart of Little Beirut, two distinct blemishes marring the beauty of an otherwise well manicured lawn.

Chapter 21

Cookies and Tracts

"Oo-ee, gooey, rich and chewy inside.
Golden, flaky, tender cakey outside.
Wrap the inside in the outside.
Is it good? Darn Tootin' Doin' the Big FIG NEWTON, the big FIG
NEWTON."

-Fig Newton Jingle-

While lying on the couch, experiencing all the wonderful symptoms of the dreaded flu, the phone started ringing. With a groan, I dislodged myself from the sofa and shuffled off towards the kitchen, and with about as much enthusiasm as a snail, lifted the phone to my face and answered, "Hello?"

"*Ahhhhhstin! Is that you?!?*" I immediately recognized the concerned, shrill voice.

"Hi, Margarite."

"Are you okay?"

"I'm ok, just a little under the weather."

If for any reason I didn't show up at Margarite Green's house on a day when she was expecting me to be on the route, she would become alarmed about my health, wonder if I had contracted malaria or some flesh-eating variant of the Bubonic plague, and then immediately call in order to make sure I hadn't died. Margarite genuinely cared about me.

"No, really, Margarite, I'm ok. I'll probably be back on the route tomorrow. Well thanks, I always appreciate your prayers. Ok, you take care too... Oh good, you'll save my cookies? Excellent. See you soon... ok, bye, bye."

The mailman predominately comes into contact with four different types of people. He runs into the ever diminishing stay-at-home mom, the second shifter, your typical unemployed bumpkin, and retired folks.

Saturday is the big exception. For it's on this day that we come into contact with the great, mowing, working class. While walking through neighborhoods filled with the pungent odor of freshly clipped grass, mailmen wave and nod at men and women bouncing along on their riders, often receiving friendly smiles in return. But we rarely chat with these people.

Numbering around 38 million, or about 12% of the American population, are those who have blown out at least sixty-five candles. And it's this group of people with whom mailmen most often interact, at least in my own personal experience.

Sitting outside in their lawn chairs, usually wearing bright yellow, or powder blue, or some plaid variation of brown pants, older men often pour over the newspaper, digesting the latest government blunder with vocal disgust. Naturally they want to share their political insights with the mailman, sometimes pontificating upon the inadequacies of health care for hours on end. But what I find especially strange is how older men will just start sharing completely random thoughts with me. While walking by Mr. Grumblemeister, he'll suddenly blurt out, "You know, they never did learn how to properly run that line."

"Excuse me?"

"Back at the old Dilling Plant, the one built by Carter Construction in fifty-five, they never did run that assembly line correctly. The managers, why they just..." And from here, Mr. Grumblemeister explores the finer points of 12 gauge wire assembly with infinite tedium, often becoming sidetracked about the history of the building and the man who was mayor at the time and a few hundred other mind-numbing facts.

One of the worst, at least with regards to talking nonstop about things that could be summed up in two sentences, was this one retired gentleman who had a habit of seeking me out while eating lunch at The Burger Barn. He always had a book with him. It would even be open. But he never read it. Instead, he spent all his time telling me about what he had already covered, unpacking the plot, nay, each paragraph with exquisite verbosity, leaving absolutely no detail untouched. Of course his books were 12,000 pages thick and required a detailed exposition of some ancient Chinese lineage in order to make sense of chapter 148.

If you're curious, it was him, in addition to farmer boy's nasty habit of stinking up the bathroom that finally led me to eat elsewhere indefinitely.

Unlike men, elderly women are far less likely to talk our ears off. If sitting outside, they're usually content to stare off into the distance and swat flies. A few who have mobility issues often request that the mail be brought inside to them. Since having become physically attached, I mean quite literally having grown human roots into the upholstery, these women sit in their recliners completely enshrouded by food trays, end tables donning books and remote controls, glasses of water, bottles of medicine and pictures of relatives who haven't visited them in months. They're usually overjoyed to see the mailman. My guess is that they go for days without human interaction.

Trying to obtain signatures from sane people can prove difficult enough, but when we're dealing with those who are in fact flirting with senility, it can be downright maddening. Mrs. Relicwrinkle, a woman born, oh, I'm going to guess around 44 A.D., is a prime example. When she looks at a certified letter, she asks with astonishment, "Oh, my, a certified letter. Who's it from?"

"It's from your bank, Mrs. Relicwrinkle. See right here?" I point to the sender.

"What do you think they want?"

"Hard to say. But if you want to find out, you need to sign here."

She looks at me like I'm trying to sucker her into signing her house over to me. "Who did you say it was from again?"

"Your bank. See right here? First Big Vault National Bank and Trust."

After scrutinizing the letter with squinty eyes for what seems like an eternity, she finally says, "I don't see anything about my bank here."

"Look right here, Mrs. Relicwrinkle." I point again, tapping the spot where she should look.

"I can't see anything. Let me get my glasses."

The elderly woman turns and starts rummaging around her living room, moving from a coffee table to a small desk to her couch at the speed of a continental drift, brushing aside knick-knacks, and mistaking a glass penguin for her glasses.

"Now where did I put those?" She mutters.

Returning finally with her reading glasses, she looks at the letter and says, "Oh, it's from my bank. Well, I can't imagine what they would want. What do you suppose they want?"

"Would you please sign these two spots?"

"Now why do I need to sign for this?"

On it goes, until finally, after much explaining and pointing and begging, Mrs. Relicwrinkle signs one of the two spots, but then, after being told that there are two spots that must be signed, she begins to wonder if this is really a good idea and starts asking about the sender afresh. One signature ends up being good enough.

If I want a real adventure, then I show up late at an assisted living complex on social security check day. In these buildings the mailboxes are usually clustered together, oftentimes set into a wall, with dozens of locked boxes neatly lined up, one next to another, almost always near, or in, the main lobby. So if I am at all running late, I can expect to see an army of mildly perturbed, white-haired men and women sitting on couches and wheelchairs, eagerly awaiting my arrival. When I enter the room, murmurings about my apparent tardiness begin to sound. Before long a wide perimeter forms around me, ensuring no escape. As I stuff the light brown, government issue envelopes into the appropriate receptacles, the ever watchful eyes of the elderly brighten with glee. Inevitably, there are always those who, whether it's from a sorting failure or some other problem, don't receive their checks. This is a very dangerous situation. Becoming enraged and tearing at their clothes like the Incredible Hulk, these once fragile citizens start hurling their aluminum walkers at my head with surprising force. Others begin wielding their canes like samurai warriors, channeling the effects of their recently ingested Viagra into their arms for added strength. A mailman's only hope at this point is to begin asking about their grandchildren. This will sometimes secure our safety.

Of all the senior citizens that I've come into contact with while delivering the mail, actually, of all the people that I've met while making my rounds, Margarite Green was my dearest patron.

While living in a small apartment on the second floor of a white duplex, near the beginning of City 15, this single, spunky, ninety-two year old woman looked upon me as a son. I should be quick to point out, however, that while I was treated like a son, truly and genuinely, I was nevertheless viewed as a wayward son, a prodigal always walking dangerously close to the crumbling edges of hell's uppermost pit. It made for a slightly dysfunctional relationship, but overall, it worked.

The origin of our relationship dates back to when I first became a regular. I can still remember our first meeting. With her door cracked ever so slightly, just wide enough for her to peer out through a thin opening, Margarite cautiously eyed me as I approached. I wasn't quite sure what to make of the defensive posture, so I tried to reassure her of my good intentions by offering up a friendly "Hello." But she didn't say anything. In fact, she narrowed her eyes. Undeterred, I called out in my friendliest voice, "Hi there."

Now you have to understand something, and it's something that my wife couldn't comprehend until she heard it for herself, but Margarite's voice was truly, and astonishingly, cartoon-like and high-pitched. If you can imagine what a female chipmunk might sound like if she could talk and if she were thrilled with having just found a large stash of nuts while being tickled and holding a megaphone, then you will have some very definite idea of Margarite's voice. When she asked me whether or not I was the new regular on the route, I hesitated for a moment. This was to allow my eardrums, which had never experienced such a strange vibration before, a moment of recovery.

After a hard blink, I said, "Yep, I'm your new mailman."

There was a curious manipulation of her mouth as she thought for a moment, and then, with a strong, sudden push, the door swung open revealing a short, wrinkly woman with bright eyes. Her hair, while obviously quite long, was pulled back and twisted around, pinned and knotted, with strands of it cascading down her back. She was wearing a long, multi-layered gown, or dress, or

171

something or other. It looked like something you might sleep in, but maybe not. It's hard to say. Whatever it was, it appeared to have been handmade in the late 1700's. It was firmly buttoned around her neck, frilly and extremely modest, with the length of the dress reaching her ankles. I would come to find out that Margarite's wardrobe consisted entirely of these gown-like dresses, though their colors varied from white to pastel in nature, each faded and a little colonial.

When her eyes looked as if they had run across a good idea, she asked if I'd be willing to ring her door bell each day and deliver the mail to her directly. She explained, "My mailbox is leaky and I don't want the mail to get wet." I looked over at the black, standard issue box. It looked weather tight to me, but I didn't make a fuss. I agreed to her request, and so from that day on it became my custom to talk with little old Margarite Green each and every day while leaning against her black iron railing.

In order to learn something of Margarite's character, one need look no further than the doorbell itself. Located just below the rectangular button and covered with a large quantity of clear tape was one great cyclopean eye, open and staring, drawn in blue ink, eyelashes pointy and long. Located directly below that, typed out in black, were the words: God Sees You. One might understand this as merely a factual statement, a truism, like "Ketchup is red," or "Bromwell is a jerk," and by so writing the phrase, the owner of the home was simply reminding her visitors of God's omniscience. But there is much more to it than that. For Margarite Green, she not only wanted people to know that God knows all, but that He also presently sees their wicked intentions.

It isn't exactly the warmest of welcomes, the kind of invitation encouraging a person to come on upstairs and enjoy some freshly baked cookies, but to understand Margarite Green, then one needs to understand that she's a fiery prophetess abounding with religious zeal.

When asked about her daily routine she would answer, "I usually pray a few hours in the morning, eat lunch, pray another couple hours, read for a while, lay down and pray, eat some supper and then go to bed around 8 o'clock."

"Wow, that's a lot of praying."

"It's my calling in life," she would confidently assert. "God has put me in this apartment so that I can pray."

"Do you really go to bed at 8 o'clock? Well then what time do you get up? 3:30 am?!? You serious?"

Margarite, above all else, was a woman of prayer. She prayed for the Mayor, the city, me, the neighbors, planes that could be heard flying overhead, everything. And when she prayed, she prayed with fervor. Especially when storms were brewing. If she heard on the radio that there was a chance of thunderstorms, she would squint and crane towards the horizon and say, "Austin, I've been praying that God would lift the storm up and take it around- cause it to miss us." That's how she always said it. "Lift it up and take it around."

The implications of her prayer never seemed to escape her notice, however, so she would often add, "Well, I'm not looking for the other cities to be hit..." there would follow a pause and some fumbling around, "so it would be better if the storm is lifted up and taken away."

When I asked what church she attended, I was told, "I follow the old holiness ways. The Pilgrim Holiness Church still follows those old ways, so that's my church."

"Who takes you to church?"

"Oh, I haven't gone in over three years."

"Three years? Why not?"

"Actually, I haven't left this apartment for at least three years."

"Are you serious?"

"I'm given over to prayer, Austin. It's God's will for my life."

"But don't you think it's God's will for you to get out and go to church?"

"Nope."

"But Margarite..."

Any attempt to convince her to the contrary proved to be an utterly futile endeavor. In the face of opposition, Margarite would set her face like flint, insisting that it was God's will for her to remain home and dedicate her life to prayer.

"What about groceries?"

"Annie brings me my groceries."

"Who's Annie?"

"One of the women from my church."

"Ok, well what about seeing other people then?"

"I have visitors from time to time."

"Don't you ever want to get out and, oh, I don't know, see the woods or the countryside?"

"Nope. My place is here."

Margarite lived a hermit's existence, and she loved it.

It took me a while to figure out what she meant by "the old ways, the old Pilgrim Holiness ways," but after about a month or two it became clear. As I continued to ring the doorbell and deliver the mail to her directly, she rewarded me with some tasty snacks. At first she gave me a variety of things, circular cookies dipped in chocolate, some tan, crunchy Girl Scout cookies, chocolate kisses and even noodles once in a while. But later on, for approximately the span of five years, each and every day, Margarite gave me a steady diet of Fig Newtons. Six to be exact. Without deviation and without fail, Margarite supplied me with, in her own words, "Bible food."

"The Bible talks about fig trees, so I thought you would appreciate some fig cookies."

She thought the apparent connection was marvelous and always chuckled at her own wit. But in addition to this "Bible food," another form of biblical nourishment was added to my diet.

"Here you go, Austin. I want you to take these."

She handed me a number of old fashioned pamphlets printed on flamboyantly colored paper. One was bright red, the other green, another shone a radiant yellow.

"What's this?"

"It's some Bible literature I want you to read."

"What's it about?"

"Worldliness."

Curious, I scanned over the material. One pamphlet explained how the King James Bible is the one, true translation. Another spoke of the sin of gambling; another appeared to be a diatribe against long hair; and yet another instructed the reader in the ways of proper attire. Opening them up, words like "Sinner" and "Repent" jumped off the page. They were italicized and written in bold type.

She asked, "Austin, do you have a King James Bible?"

"I do, but that isn't the one I read," I began. "I prefer more readable translations."

Margarite suddenly looked as if she was going into a swoon. She began rocking back and forth, almost as if the very ground under her feet were quaking. With one hand she gripped the railing and with the other she clutched some invisible object in the air. And then her mouth opened wide and there followed a tremendous gasping sound like that of drowning man struggling for air.

I took a step back.

"Austin, what do you mean you don't read the King James Bible? That's the Word of God! Don't you believe in the Word of God?"

"I do, Margarite, but it's not like the King James Version is the only true translation out there. There are other good ones, you know."

Margarite's head drooped low, and then slowly, and quite mournfully, it shook back and forth with all the gloom of a funeral procession. While staring down at the ground, she began to inform me about "those modern translations," and how they are works of the devil, meant to mislead people and water down God's Word.

I tried to explain that the New Testament was originally written in Greek and that it could be translated into English without all the "Thee's" and "Thou's" and other such archaic components common to old English speech. But this had no effect upon her. Instead, she declared with infinite conviction that she only wanted to read the Bible that the apostle Paul carried around with him, and that those who tamper with God's Word can expect to be damned.

I would also come to find out that she thought of anyone with a beard as thoroughly pagan. And if it happened that the person with the beard also wore shorts, or if they owned shorts, or even approved of shorts, then this was a tell-tale sign that they were irredeemably conquered and controlled by the armies of darkness.

I can't say that I've ever grown a full-blown beard, certainly some lazy scruff now and then, but nothing that would be considered purposeful or bushy. So this scored quite a few sanctification points in her eyes. But I wore shorts when it got hot, and so this caused Margarite to twitch a little, though she usually considered my wearing such ungodly apparel as somewhat of an exception to her rule, mostly because she liked me and partly because I looked as if I was about to die when it got up to around ninety-five degrees.

In addition to these heathen practices, she also condemned playing cards, owning a television (but not a phone), wearing jewelry, drinking alcohol of any kind, amusement parks (don't ask why), rock and roll, fireworks (they are a waste of money), and many other things. All of these things, if practiced or condoned, are sure marks of the lost and produce within Margarite an acute, volcanic indignation, the explosion of which manifests itself in a vibrant array of horrified expressions.

Like the Caroways, and, at least in my experience, about eighty percent of senior citizens, Margarite harbored racist tendencies. It wasn't as if she thought of herself as racially superior to Hispanics, or that she thought of herself as intrinsically more valuable than they were, that would be misstating the case, but that Mexicans were simply strange creatures who ate bizarre, smelly foods, spoke in gibberish and played loud, devilish music. She was basically paranoid that they were secretly plotting her demise or possibly sacrificing children to the pagan god Molek. Her not being able to understand what they were saying contributed greatly to her misconceptions. I'm pretty sure that she confused the smells of their spicy foods with incense, their foreign speech with incantations and their music with carnal beats designed to work the mind into an altered state of otherworldly consciousness. I tried to assure her that none of this was true, but she would still watch them closely from out her window, eyeing them fearfully as they tossed chicken on their grill.

Margarite was a living paradox. She was generous, yet legalistic; obstinate, yet sweet. She gave, but demanded; preached, but never left her home. She could be motherly, and yet alienate. Margarite's faith was also unshakable, but unfortunately marred with ignorance and preserved by stubbornness. We would sometimes argue at length over doctrinal issues, no doubt perplexing the neighbors as they would hear us debating over the true nature of grace and practical holiness. But no matter how prodigal I became in her eyes, and no matter how much she frustrated me, the two of us continued to put up with one another, even enjoying each other's company, amazingly enough. For just about the time I couldn't bear another moment of her unreasonable dogmatism, her quirky, endearing side would shine through.

To mention one such occasion, she once invited me up to her apartment to look at some old photographs. When we reached the top of her stairs, she turned around and exclaimed in amazement, "Why, Austin, you're a giant!" Up until that moment, she thought I was an inch or two shorter than she because I had always stood at the bottom of the two steps leading up to her door while talking to her. But when we finally stood on level ground in her living room, I suddenly towered over her five-foot two frame. She could hardly believe it, but felt a certain measure of relief actually. She said, "I always thought you were terribly short and felt bad for you."

Margarite also made sure to call me on Christmas day. When I, or my wife, would pick up the phone, she would shriek, "MERRY CHRISTMAS!" I think my wife was the first to receive one of her holiday proclamations. She initially thought it was a prank call, given the wildly intense and unfamiliar voice of Margarite.

Despite all her frustrating idiosyncrasies, I couldn't help but like Mrs. Green. And that's part of the joy of being a regular. We're forced to interact with people we might otherwise avoid, maybe even run from. But once in a while a surprising relationship emerges from the pool of random encounters. That's what happened with Margarite Green. She was the little old lady at 919 ½ East Wheeler Street who invariably provided me with six Fig Newtons, a healthy supply of Pilgrim Holiness tracts, and a large quantity of paradoxical love.

Chapter 22

Watch Out! The Owners Bite Too!

"Two spoiled rotten dogs live here."

-A sign over a mailbox-

Judging from the way the vein bulged on the side of the bald man's head, I thought it prudent to take seriously his threats of bodily harm.

"Look," I shouted, "just get~ Hey! Get him back~ Back, dang it!"

The dog went for my feet again.

"You'd better not hurt him!" exclaimed the bald man, quickly adding, "Champ! Get over~ Don't you dare spray him, mailman! Put it down or else I'm gonna..." As the weight of the man's spherical body tilted forward, his two stubby legs pumped hard, but only momentarily. The entire movement was meant to feign a charge. Waving frantically, he shouted, "He don't bite! Stop! He don't bite!"

The man yelling at me was a Mr. Randy Guntry, a ticked off, short, stout man with a bright red, chubby face. (In an attempt to be charitable, I have sought to downplay his rather rotund physique by replacing the word 'portly' with the more congenial term 'stout.' Other than that, the rest of the description is quite accurate).

Mr. Guntry lives at the end of a sleepy street in a normally quiet neighborhood. The only time things liven up is when his dog, a small, light brown pinscher with an unusually small head, tries to slam through Randy's storm door in an attempt to gnaw on the mailman's leg. Inside, on the couch, within view of the mailbox, Mr. Guntry enjoys his dog's theatrics with a toothy grin. The sound of laughing that can sometimes be heard spilling out from his mouth, no doubt in response to his dog's loony bravado, is one of mirth, the kind originating from somewhere deep within his stouter regions. I wouldn't hold it against someone if they confused Randy's laugh with Jabba the Hut's.

Rumor has it that Mr. Guntry likes to lounge around his house, and preferably upon the couch, in the nude. Since he's in plain view of the porch, some of the female carriers have been offended by the sight and have lodged complaints against him, passionately calling him a dirty perv, as well as a few other choice words. I've never personally ventured a lingering look, but have only perceived the general outline of something fleshy from out of the corner of my eye, which was plenty enough for me.

There have been those who have disputed the accusation, saying that he's only partially nude, maintaining that his equipment is in fact concealed behind a pair of whitey tighties. "It's all in the angle," they point out. "If you're viewing the man from the wrong angle you can easily lose sight of the underwear and conclude that he's naked. But you've got to tilt your head a bit, or scoot over slightly, then you'll see 'em." Not everyone has been convinced by this observation, and so the question is still very much open to debate.

On this particular midsummer afternoon, while approaching Mr. Guntry's house, I noticed that his pincher was loose in the front yard. The dog was sniffing around for a spot to do its business. Mr. Guntry sat reclined on his porch, courageously testing the limits of his wooden swing. When the dog spotted me, it instantly charged. The situation instantly turned sour. As I yelled and kicked at the mutt, trying to keep it at bay until I could whip out my mace and light him up, Mr. Guntry lumbered over to his dog's rescue, shouting out threats that if I so much as touched his dog, he would inflict serious bodily harm upon me. This was more than a little unnerving. Not only was I trying to keep his dog, which continued to dart in with flashing teeth, from biting me, but I had to try to carry on a conversation with a man who was every bit as threatening as his snapping dog.

"Just get your dog back," I tried to explain again, while aiming my mace at the pincher's face, "and everything will turn out just fine."

For some inexplicable reason, rather than grabbing his dog, he chose instead to stand behind Champ with clinched fists and shout, "I'm telling you, mailman, he don't bite! Just leave him alone! He don't bite!"

In the course of his daily travels, the mailman hears a number of oft repeated questions from his patrons. When it's cold, he's asked, "Is it cold enough for ya, mailman?" Conversely, when it's hot, they ask, "Is it hot enough for ya?" When you are suffering from heat exhaustion and on the verge of throwing up your lime green Gatorade, a simple "yes" seems hardly sufficient, let alone necessary. But many carriers nevertheless smile and offer up a polite chuckle, responding, "Oh, yes, it's plenty warm," or, "It is cold, isn't it?" Some of the more comedic carriers, like Jerry- the one you may recall who affectionately refers to me as a boil- will generate a goofy grin and say, "You can't tell, ma'am, but it's like February in my shorts right now." In the winter he also gets a kick out of telling people, "Right here under this sock cap, yep, this one right here, it's just like I'm lying out on the beach in Florida."

By far the most common theme we mailmen hear is, "You can keep the bills," or, "If it ain't a check, just keep on going," or, "Now don't leave any bills, ok?" What is especially striking about these oft-repeated statements is how people act as though they're really clever and chuckle heartily, almost as if something genuinely funny were just discovered and uttered for the first time. It never occurs to them that maybe, just maybe, we have already heard the phrase a few thousand times that afternoon and therefore find it a little difficult to act tickled. For some, they say it in a tone that makes one wonder if they really mean for you to keep their bills, "No seriously, I'm quite willing and in fact want you to take my bills and conveniently lose them. Right there's a river. Go on. Do it." For yet others, the statement is nothing more than a habit, a phrase they feel compelled, for some mysterious reason, to repeat over and over again.

One guy near the outskirts of Little Beirut will, without fail and without variation, self-amusingly quip, "You can keep the bills...." (Next day) "You can keep the bills..." (Next day) "You can keep the bills..." Ad infinitum. What am I supposed to say to that?

"Um, I can't?"   "Uh, I don't want them?"   Or, "Uh, what's wrong with you?"

Although this next statement isn't heard quite as frequently as "You can keep the bills," it should undoubtedly be ranked among the top four things a mailman most often hears.   Randy said it earlier. He declared, "He don't bite!"

Mailmen are constantly told, "Don't worry, he doesn't bite," or, "Don't worry, he wouldn't hurt a fly," or, "Oh, don't worry, he's all bark and no bite."   Please believe me when I tell you that I'm not exaggerating this point, but dog owners truly believe that their dogs are pacifists by nature, merely long-nosed Quakers looking to lead quiet and peaceful lives.   They firmly believe that when their dogs are literally going berserk, doing everything possible to break free and tackle me, it's merely because- and yes, I've heard this many, many times- they simply want to lick me to death, or play, or get to know me, or just sniff my hand.   Their dog could be a hundred and forty pounds, foaming, lunging at my leg and they will still insist that their pet most certainly, and without exception, will not bite. "Never mind the fact," they say, "that my dog's already ripped off one of your arms and firmly latched onto your face.   No, no, don't worry.   Take comfort!   My dog has absolutely no intention of hurting you.   He's a good dog."

Why dog owners almost universally believe such craziness is a complete mystery to me.   They will freely admit that other dogs do in fact bite.   And they will confess that their dog *looks* like it wants to bite.   And they will readily acknowledge that their dog has a powerful mandible that's capable of clamping shut, a motion that *seems* to resemble the operation of biting.   But lo', they will still insist that their dog, unlike every other land shark, does not bite.

My personal favorite is when someone tries to convince me that their pit bull is harmless.   The owner confidently asserts that his dog is misunderstood and harbors only the kindest of intentions.   Of course while he's saying this, the pit bull, who's standing slightly behind his master and just off to one side, is pointing at me, silently mouthing, "I'm gonna kill you."

This is very disturbing.

But mailmen love to joke about all of this.   One of the old timers I used to work with, a guy we called Big Daddy, had a fondness for acting out the interplay between mailmen, dog owners and their dogs. He played each part masterfully. While standing out on the workroom floor, he begins, "Oh, don't worry mailman, I can assure you that my dog would never bite you." And then, with a suddenness that startles the unprepared, he instantly turns into a maniacal, snapping dog bent on tearing apart the mailman, who he then becomes, leg extended, jiggling as if the dog were securely fastened to it. Add to this the terrible sounds of gurgling, which is supposed to be the mailman dying, as well as, "Rahrrrrr-snarl-snort-rip-doggy laugh," and everyone bursts out in laughter, applauding heartily. It's a beautiful performance.

So when Mr. Guntry tried to assure me that his dog "don't bite," he merely expressed what all other dog owners have said in similar situations. Well, not like *every* dog owner out there. There was this one elderly woman who stepped out onto her porch, looked over at her crazy, yapping mutt which was tied up to a tree and said, "Listen, mailman, he'll bite ya if given the chance. Watch out for him." At that moment a light shone out of heaven upon her and I heard what sounded like angels singing. I don't remember much of anything after that. I think I blacked out.

Well, anyway, Randy wasn't acting abnormally at all when he claimed his dog didn't bite. But neither was he acting strangely when he threatened me with physical violence. That's quite normal too. You see, dog owners are fiercely protective of their pets, even when their animal is clearly trying to kill a human being. They're so zealous for their furry delinquents, in fact, that I'm almost convinced that some dogs are capable of casting powerful spells upon their owners so as to charm them into thinking that they are equal in worth to humans- no, more than that- that they are in fact one of their own offspring, certainly furrier, but loved just the same. Seem hard to believe? Then consider this: In 2004, the American Animal Hospital Association, a professional veterinary association of more than 33,000 veterinary care providers, provided 1,238 dog owners with a questionnaire. The three dozen or so questions on the questionnaire touched upon a broad assortment of subjects. Some of the questions were basic, such as: "What state do you live in?" But others were far more specific, like: "How much have you spent on veterinary care for your pet during the past 12 months?"

Allow me to cite a few of the results:

Question 4: If you were deserted on an island and could have only one companion, which would you pick?

Human 47%
Dog...40%
Cat 10%
Other..02%
None..<01%

Question 9a: How likely are you to risk your own life for your pet?

Very likely 56%
Somewhat likely 37%
Not at all likely..07%

Question 12: Who listens to you best?

Pet...45%
Spouse/significant other 30%
Friend 11%
Family member..11%
Other 03%

Question 16: How often do you think of your pet while you are away from him or her during the day?

All the time 21%
Every hour 7%
A few times per day 54%
Once a day 13%
Never 3%
I am never away from my pet during the day..........2%

As should be plain, most dog owners are terribly confused and firmly held captive by their dog's magical powers (Unless of course you are a dog owner yourself, then you are asking, "What? What's wrong with these results?").

Dog owners love their dogs like children, maybe even more than their children. And so when the mailman is attacked by a dog when the owner is around, the situation inevitably turns ugly, for the owner considers an assault on their dog as equal in heinosity to an assault on one of their children. It's true. People have cussed me out, threatened me, called the post office to file a complaint and have become almost as enraged as the elderly when they don't receive their Social Security checks.

Hysteria isn't all that uncommon either. I once had to deal with a woman who kept screaming in horror as she watched me fend off her angry chow. While covering her face and bouncing up and down, she kept crying out, "Don't spray him! (Scream!) He's a good dog! (Scream)!" You might have thought that I was preparing to set off a nuclear bomb by her reaction. All the commotion alerted her husband, and so a moment later he burst out the front door, face marked with concern, wanting to know what was going on. His wife told him that I was threatening her; that I was demanding that she put the dog up or else. I had spoken firmly, but threaten her? Not at all.

Naturally, the husband went ape, rearing over me like a grizzly bear, yelling, "You threatening my wife! You wanna hurt my dog, mailman!" I did manage to escape without suffering injury to my face. Of course he did call the post office, telling them that I threatened his wife. That made for a fun afternoon.

One other time I rounded the corner of a house and found myself face to face with a large boxer. Both the dog and I were completely taken by surprise. I immediately began back peddling, fumbling around for my mace. The sudden motion startled the dog and so he charged, snapping at my shoes as I continued my retreat. When I snatched my dog mace and began spraying him down, my finger slipped a little too far forward, half covering the hole where the juice shoots out, causing, as anyone who has ever pressed their thumb over the end of a garden hose can testify, the stream to spurt everywhere. So orange pepper spray shot out in all directions, hitting both the dog and me, but mostly me, and in the face. But that's not all. As I continued to back pedal, moving as fast as I could, I slammed into a wheel barrel full of rocks. It caught me right behind the knees. It was a perfect leg sweep. I tumbled backwards, saw my black sneakers against the blue sky and landed with a star studded "thump." The wheel barrel toppled over as well, spilling rocks everywhere, not the least on me. Slightly dazed and unable to see clearly because of the intense burning, I tried to locate the boxer. He was gone. But at that moment, a man with strange tattoos all over his arms emerged from the house. Running over to me he said, "What the hell happened, man?" Working my way back to my feet, rubbing my eyes with my shirt, I proceeded to tell him that his boxer tried to bite me. "No, no," he assured me, "that dog doesn't bite. He just wanted to sniff you." And then with his hands on his hips, "You didn't need to go and spray him, man." I shot him a sharp look, "You're kidding, right? Look, I walked around the corner and your dog came right for me, snapping at my feet."

It didn't matter what I said, he continued to insist that his dog was a saint. When I began rubbing the back of my legs where I nailed the wheel barrel, he politely asked, "Are you ok?" But when I hesitated, his tone quickly changed. He said, "Don't be a freaking pussy cat." (Only he didn't use the word freaking and didn't say anything at all about a cat.) If my vision hadn't been so blurry, I'm sure I would have seen red at that moment.

"Excuse me?" I said, voice trembling.

"You heard me. Quit being a freaking pussy cat."

I had to summon every last ounce of self-restraint in order to keep myself from clubbing him with the toppled wheel barrel. Needless to say, I was seriously ticked off.

But never mind about how I felt. The point is this: Dog owners clearly experience some kind of mental glitch when we mailmen have to protect ourselves from their feisty vermin. It's as if something snaps within them and they lose their minds. It's like what I said earlier, pets are merely hairy children.

Some of you who own a dog may have never witnessed your pet attack a mailman, and so you may be wondering how you might respond to a situation where the mailman has to defend himself. Most like to think that they would never lash out in violence, but they can't be entirely sure. As a professional, I would like to help you determine just how likely you are to lose your cool, in the event of your dog being sprayed with mace.

Follow this exercise.

I want you to first imagine that it's a fine summer day, so fine in fact, that you have opened the front door, allowing sunlight to pour in through your glass storm door. Now imagine that the storm door isn't fully latched shut. At the sound of mail being dropped into your mailbox, your sweet little Muffin perks up, dashes off, slams into the door and finds himself outside, having successfully pushed his way past. Leaping off the couch, you run to the door just in time to call out, "Don't worry, mailman, my dog doesn't bite." But it's too late. You watch the mailman whip out his pepper spray and douse your little Muffin with a generous quantity of orange repellant. And right in the face.

Answer honestly now. How do you think you would respond?

Would you:

1.   Applaud the mailman for protecting himself from your dog, thus insuring that you won't be sued, or have to pay for any hospital bills, or possibly have to put your little Muffin to sleep?

2.   Feel slightly annoyed, but still recognize that the mailman didn't have any other choice?

3.   Express disappointment and even some anger, but refrain from showing excessive emotion?

4.   Express your contempt for the mailman by weaving together a host of rare and exotic profanities?

5.   Look for a blunt object, maybe one of your lawn ornaments, with which to beat the mailman?

If you answered one, two or three, then you are hopelessly self-deceived. If you answered number four, then you are close to the truth and should feel good about your self-awareness. Merely add number five to your answer and you will be only inches away from true reality.

But in order to determine more precisely how likely you are (an actual percentage) of acting out numbers four and five, answer the following questions:

Yes or No

1.   Do you think it's cute when your dog jumps on company?
2.   Are there pictures of your dog in the family photo album?
3.   Did you cry while watching or reading Old Yeller?
4.   Do you own two or more dogs?
5.   Do you think your dog is going to heaven when it dies?
6.   Do you feed your dog on a regular basis?

If you answered yes to any of these questions, then there is a 99.9% chance that you will want to beat your mailman, if he ever has to spray or kick your dog.

So as anyone can see, Mr. Guntry was acting in a totally normal and predictable manner when he came to his dog's rescue.

Back to Mr. Guntry now. After more heated dialogue and more dexterous foot work on my part, Randy finally shouted out, "Just leave! I don't care about my mail. Just get out of here!"

I was more than obliged.

So away I went, walking backwards, slowly edging away from the sinister mutt until I was well off Randy's property.

When I returned back to the post office, a suspicious supervisor greeted me. He expressed concern over a phone call he had received from an irate patron. "A Mr. Guntry," he began, "You know him? Yes, I see. Well, he said that you were threatening to hurt his dog."

That's usually how it goes. If for some reason there is an unfortunate altercation between someone's dog and their mailman, the owner will, almost without fail, call in and claim that it was the mailman who instigated the fight and committed war crimes against their Muffin, claiming that he utilized biological warfare or practiced torture on their poor animal.

Rarely is this true.

After explaining my side of the story, the supervisor asked one simple question, "Are you sure that his dog wasn't on a leash?"

They ask this question because it's the million dollar question. If a dog isn't on its leash, then the mailman isn't at fault (so long as he doesn't drop kick the owner or unnecessarily harm the animal). Basically, a loose dog isn't an innocent dog, according to most leash laws. So naturally, we urge people to tie up their dogs, to make sure that they are securely fastened far away from the mailbox. But of course dog owners would never tie up one of their children to a tree, now would they?

Chapter 23

Time to Eat

"It requires a certain kind of mind to see beauty in a hamburger bun. Yet is it any more unusual to find grace in the texture and softly carved silhouette of a bun than to reflect lovingly on the hackles of a fishing fly? Or the arrangements and textures on a butterfly's wing? Not if you are a McDonalds's man."

-Ray Kroc, creator of the McDonald's franchise-

————————————

There is a space of time between 11:30AM and 1:00PM when the good order of society is abandoned and replaced with the laws of tooth and claw. We commonly refer to this phenomenon as lunch. It is during this time when working men and women leave their place of employment in search of food, scrambling off to fast food joints, clawing their way through the masses, biting and pushing their way to a register, doing whatever is necessary to fill their bellies with beefy sustenance, and all within the span of thirty minutes, or maybe an hour, if they are very special.

Because the mailman must also eat, he too engages in the practice of lunch. So around 12:15 pm, I typically head off for McDonald's.

I don't know why I keep going to McDonald's, but I do. For if there's one place that should be avoided at all costs, if there is one place that can drive a person to insanity, or committing acts of violence, it has to be McDonald's during a lunch rush. It's like I'm a crack addict, though I fill my veins with McChicken sandwiches and double cheeseburgers, or anything and everything else on the dollar menu. But it's not just me. There are thousands, no there are billions who are equally as addicted. And stupid.

So like these countless others, I endure the hardships and frustrations of McDonald's, subjecting myself to the same greasy gauntlet over and over again, swearing on one day that I will never go back, but then, the next day, returning like a true McMasochist.

The lunch experience really begins to take shape once a parking spot has been found. There is a striking resemblance between the video game Frogger and the person trying to make it to the front entrance. Wild-eyed luncheonites zoom to and fro in search of a free space, careening around corners, low blood sugar dulling their senses but heightening their road rage. Only a novice would recommend taking one's time while hopping across the parking lot. Speed is of the essence, because everything depends upon reaching the McDonald's entrance before others do. This is crucial.

There is always that moment, while locking up my truck, when I survey my surroundings and catch sight of someone, not too far away, rising from their vehicle. It's a businessman on his lunch break. Our gazes meet, and there is a quick glance towards the entrance, and then a flash of contemplation. He is calculating our respective distances from that door.

Although neither of us betray any signs of panic, and even though both of our strides appear balanced and casual, we walk as quickly as is humanly possible towards that door without looking like we are trying to beat the other. The reason is simple. If he makes it to the register before I do, then I have to wait that much longer, thus diminishing precious lunch time.

One has to be careful though. If I reach the door right before he does, then I'm faced with a tough decision. Will I go ahead and impolitely jump on through or will I courteously open the door and allow him to go first? If it's a woman or an older man, I'm pretty much obligated to open the door for them. So in those cases, one needs to make sure that they arrive at the entrance four seconds ahead of them. Anything under four seconds obligates a gentleman to hold open the door. It's only right, after all. However, older men tend to be slow and women hinder their mobility by wearing high heels, so the four second rule isn't too difficult to achieve.

And remember that you can sprint around to side doors, if they happen to be trailing you closely.

Returning to the businessman, if you reach the door before he does, and he's right on your heels, then I recommend utilizing the forward moving prop technique. You simply enter ahead of him, but lean back, propping the door open with an extended arm, thus allowing him to grab a hold of it. This maneuver secures your lead, while also exhibiting a measure of courtesy. If executed correctly, he will also feel obligated to thank you. It's very effective.

Making it inside McDonald's in good time can be a very rewarding experience, but it is often short lived. For once inside, the sight of a long, disheveled, snaking line, filled with foot-tapping, arm crossed, disgruntled luncheonites quickly dispels any notion of victory.

As the hungry throng impatiently waits, McDonald's employees can be seen scrambling about, some dropping fries, others tossing cheeseburgers into drive through sacks, a few staring hopelessly at monitors. Over the frantic sounds of deep fryers beeping and buzzing, manager's can be heard shouting, "I need that Quarter, no pickle, now! And give me a ten-three run of doubles. No, let the phone ring. Just leave it. Someone get me that sandwich for drive-through. Hurry up!"

There are four registers, but only two are running. This is the next crucial moment in the lunch experience. It is a question of which line to choose. Will you go with the line on the right, or the line on the left?

If you watch and listen carefully, important clues will present themselves as to which line is most advantageous. A young woman, her badge reads, Clarissa, is working the left register. She is punching in the orders confidently and deftly flipping out trays with the appropriate cups. The register on the right is operated by a slightly older woman. Her badge reads, Tina. While staring at her register, fingertip floating around, hovering inches over the screen, she can be heard muttering, "Now where's the add cheese button, I know it's here somewhere, um, cheese, cheese..."

You have to be quick, for when these words are uttered, people begin diving into the other line. A distracted mother with squawking children, an elderly woman with diminished hearing, and a businessman speaking loudly on his cell phone are all that remain in line Tina. Those in line Clarissa regard them with pity.

Something remarkable happens while standing in line. People may not realize it, but McDonald's unites complete strangers in a common cause. I don't care if it's the man holding a briefcase with a blue tooth wrapped around his ear, or if it's the grubby roofers with measuring tapes hooked to their belts, McDonald's unites them all together in a grand and electric frustration. Only waiting thirteen minutes for a supersized number three can do that.

So thank you, McDonald's. Thank you for bringing us all together.

Watching people wait for their food is never boring. One can literally see blood pressures rising. And it's always interesting to observe how different people deal with the building anger. Some rock back and forth on their heels, others lean against the wall with a look of disgust, and a few vocalize their irritation. Speaking to no one in particular, one announces, "This is unbelievable! What's wrong with these people?" Others quietly share their plight with the person standing next to them, murmuring incomplete thoughts, "You know, I don't understand- just can't they once, I mean really, one time, just one time..."

There must be something special in the food to keep so many people coming back, day after day, incomplete order after incomplete order. Someday we'll probably learn that aliens have taken over McDonald's, and that they were slipping some kind of alluring drug into the Big Mac sauce. This would actually go a long way in explaining why there are so many strange people working at McDonald's. They are just aliens in disguise, struggling to learn our language and operate our machinery. This might also explain the high turnover rate too. Maybe the aliens take some of the human employees up to their mother ship and perform experiments upon them? Or maybe these people are liquefied and used to form the special ingredient in the Big Mac sauce? If this last suggestion bothers you, then just imagine that the people aren't liquefied, but are rather made slaves on the planet McLunarnugget, forced to work in one of the alien factories where the secret sauce is made.

Is there a better explanation?

Carriers often each lunch together and in small packs. There are of course those who prefer to eat alone, but for many, the chance to come together and dine, not only on a tasty burger, but on juicy gossip, is too good to pass up.

Most of the groups have a set rotation for lunch. On Monday, it's understood that they will eat at Subway. Tuesday, Wendy's. And so on and so forth. The group that I often met up with, before several of them retired, utilized a more patriarchal approach for determining where to eat. At some point in the morning, one of the guys would call out, "Hey, Big Daddy! Where we eatin'?" Turning around to face the open workroom floor, long, gray pony tail swinging gently behind him, Big Daddy, the oldest mailman in our Post Office, would rub his chin and ponder the question thoughtfully. When his mind was made up, he would, like a Chieftain addressing his tribe, announce his verdict, usually selecting Burger Barn or McDonald's as the ideal location for clogging our arteries.

After successfully navigating our way through the painful process of obtaining food, we would sit together and, like thousands of other carriers scattered across the nation, pontificate upon the awful deeds of postal management. It's a nearly irresistible temptation for mailmen to do this. But not all are equally as obsessive. There are those whose very happiness, those whose very existence, depends upon them having an audience with which to air the ineptitudes of their boss.

"Two Guys" is definitely one such person. He loved to work up a good sweat while blasting away at management, often using spare napkins, his sleeve or anything else absorbent to mop up his leaky forehead. Actually, he didn't need to get fired up in order to begin perspiring profusely. He has been known to literally soak his winter parka through with sweat, while delivering the mail in single digit temperatures. One time a dermatologist even called the Post Office to complain about his sweaty diffusions. Apparently the doctor's mail was so thoroughly drenched that even he, a skin specialist, couldn't restrain feelings of disgust. Management politely asked "Two Guys" to try to keep the mail away from his body.

Fortunately, the guys I used to eat lunch with weren't quite so manic about management and usually channeled their frustrations through the medium of humor, choosing to laugh away their concerns rather than risk suffering an aneurism due to excessive venting. One of the old timers, a man by the name of John Blast, was a first rate comedian in this respect. He would have us clutching our sides with laughter, reduced to tears in no time.

"Blast" wasn't really his last name, but merely an apt nickname given to him for his unique ability to fart on command. Naturally, most of the female carriers were anything but impressed by this talent, let alone amused, but the men adored him. They looked upon him as someone special, someone gifted. Legendary.

Early on in my career, John Blast took a liking to me, choosing to refer to me not as Brownie, or simply Austin, but rather, "One stripe." "If we slapped a White Sox uniform on Austin, it would only have one stripe," he would say, referring to my slender build. The nickname "One stripe" didn't last long, however. When I received my first dog bite, some of the carriers started calling me "Milkbone." "Just look at those skinny, white legs." they chuckled. "Can't blame the dog, really. Probably thought he was looking at two tasty bones."

Honestly, I couldn't blame the dog. He was asleep underneath a porch swing and I didn't have the faintest idea he was under there. When he woke up, my two exposed, white legs were dangling right before his eyes. Shoot, the dog probably thought he was still dreaming. Whatever the case, he chomped into my calf and ran off, leaving me with his signature: Three holes.

It wasn't long before people in my community started referring to me as Milkbone. It all began when someone from the local newspaper dropped by the Post Office to write a story about dog bites. When the reporter requested to speak with two or three carriers, a number of my beloved co-workers began pointing excitedly in my direction, "Yeah, talk to Milkbone over there- that guy right there, the one with the milky legs." When the story hit the paper, complete strangers would call out, "Hey, aren't you that mailman they call Milkbone? Ha, ha, Milkbone, huh? Too funny, man."

While everyone liked John Blast, not everyone believed he was all there. According to patrons on his route, they said he would just start cussing for no reason in particular, almost as if he were suffering from Tourettes syndrome. People on his route reported, "No really, I was watching him out my window, and all of a sudden, he started cussing, and I mean he was cussing! "F" this, "Sonsa" that- I'm telling you, mailman, something's wrong with that guy."

Maybe something was wrong with him. That's possible. But ask any mailman to list off the top three or four things that really annoy him, and they will probably say- after mentioning management, dogs and getting pie- dropping a letter. When you have to bend over to pick up a letter, one that continues to flip away in the wind when your fingers are inches away from it, and then, once you get a hold of the thing, straighten up your back with a heavy bag strapped across your chest, it's strangely infuriating. Maybe John dropped a lot of letters? Who knows? It's been a mystery for years.

Either way, everyone at my Post Office liked John, except maybe this one Postmaster named Gregory. In the course of daily postal life, it became popular to take something someone would say and turn it into a lighthearted slam by inserting the word "this" at a strategic location. So if someone were to ask, for example, "Hey, Bill, can you bundle out that pie for me?" Bill would crack, "Ah, bundle this!" The snappy retort would receive a few chuckles, and then Bill would happily bundle out the mail. Well on this one day when Gregory, a Postmaster who normally hid out in his office, just happened to be walking across the workroom floor at a moment when we were talking and joking around too loudly, he sternly commanded, "Hold it down!" Since John's back was facing the Postmaster, and since he was quick on the draw when it came to the "this" game, he called back, "Hold *this* down!" John's words hit the air at the precise moment when everyone else suddenly grew silent. I can still vividly remember the way in which the Postmaster jerked to a sudden stop and then turned slowly towards John, glaring furiously. Even if the Postmaster didn't recognize John's voice, it would have been easy for him to figure out who said it, for every head in that building was whipping back and forth, first looking at the Postmaster, then at John, back to the Postmaster and then, with complete wonder, back at John. The words, "What did you say?" crawled out of the Postmaster's mouth like four stalking panthers.

I'm not sure I have ever seen a person stammer quite as severely as John at that moment.

It isn't uncommon for mailmen to receive yummy snacks from their patrons. There are those who set out a plate of cookies or homemade chocolates by the mailbox with a folded note, "For the mailman." It's a wonderful gesture, and most mailmen gladly carry off the tasty morsels and nibble on them throughout the day. I'd like to enjoy them. I really would. But I just can't. The simple truth is that I'm paranoid. When I look down at the cookies, I certainly see the colorful sprinkles and the glistening sugar and feel a certain allure, but I can't help but wonder what nasties might be lurking within. I can't help but picture Mrs. Opensore kneading her dough, humming, completely unaware that ooze from one of her blisters is dripping into the mix. So try as I might, I can't bring myself to eating anything that isn't prepackaged. Margarite is the only exception, and even then it took me a while before I could muster up the courage to eat food she had handled.

The same is true with drinks. People are always offering drinks to letter carriers when it's hot. Sometimes a tall glass of water will be sitting out for us, a bead of cool condensation streaking down the side. It's so inviting, and most don't hesitate to gulp it down. But no sooner will I convince myself that it's ok, when I'll notice one tiny, almost imperceptible floatie swirling around the bottom of the glass. It looks like a sea monkey, or maybe a flake of skin. Whatever it is, I can't bring myself to drinking it, not even a sip. But I can't simply leave it there either. That would be rude. So looking around cautiously, I pour the water out into a nearby bush and then quickly put it back, maybe even letting out a loud, "Ahhhh." Problem solved. But once in a while a patron will come to the door, holding a glass of water in their hand. "Here you go, mailman," they say. "I thought you might want something refreshing." They then smile and offer it with an extended arm. This is a difficult situation. But even here there is a respectable way out. I'll accept the glass of water, look upon it thoughtfully and then say, "You know what I would really like to do with this ice cold water?" They shrug their shoulders. "I would really like to pour this refreshing drink on my head. That would feel really good about right now. No, no, I've got plenty of water back at my truck, just let me- Ahhhh- there, oh that felt wonderful. Wow, thank you. I really needed that." And then I hand the drink back.

I'm even hesitant to drink from certain pop cans. It's not the pop can, per say, but what might be on the pop can. There's this one guy who likes to zip around on a red moped. Every now and then he'll bring me a fresh, unopened can of Coca-Cola. Again, it's a magnanimous gesture, but he has the kind of face that says he likes to play a lot Dungeons and Dragons and might even like to pretend, once in a while, that he's a fourteenth level druid warrior. I simply can't help but wonder what peculiar substance might have found its way onto the lip of the soda can.

Don't misunderstand me though. We mailmen love to receive these kinds of gifts. Like I've said already, most carriers gobble this stuff up without a care in the world. They lick the chocolate off each finger, not the least bit concerned about their having handled hundreds of germ infested letters- letters sent from other countries- letters that no doubt have monkey poo on them. That's fine. Let them eat their snacks. I'll gratefully receive my own goodies and then, later on, toss the questionable treats into the mouths of yappy dogs.

Chapter 24

The Last Enemy

"O death, where is your victory? O death, where is your sting?" The sting of death is sin, and the power of sin is the law. But thanks be to God, who gives us the victory through our Lord Jesus Christ.

-The Apostle Paul-

It was taking Margarite longer than usual to answer the door. I didn't think anything of it at first. Sometimes it simply took a while. So while leaning comfortably on the iron railing, staring blankly at some riding toys in the neighbor's yard, I patiently waited on the steps.

More time went by.

Maybe she didn't hear the doorbell? Or maybe, I pondered further, *maybe, she's talking to someone important on the phone and can't let them go.* I had no idea who that might be, but thought it possible. *Maybe she went somewhere?* I dismissed the thought as soon as it entered my mind. A woman who hasn't left her apartment in over five years just doesn't up and leave without mentioning it. She surely would have said something. My finger moved towards the doorbell again, but was caught short by the distant sound of footsteps.

Ah, there she is.

A few moments later, Margarite answered the door. She looked pale and weak. Something was clearly wrong.

"Are you ok, Margarite?" I asked, moving forward.

Normally she would push the storm door open and chat, but not today. She stood on the bottom step, gripping the hand railing, trying to keep her balance. When I opened the door, I asked if she was alright again. With a shaky voice she quietly answered, "Austin, I'm just so weak."

"Are you sick?"

"It must be the flu," She began. "Oh, Austin, I'm just so terribly weak." She continued to lean heavily on the railing.

"Margarite, you shouldn't have come down these stairs."

She shook her head, "No, no, I wanted to give you your cookies." She extended her hand, offering me a bag filled with six Fig Newtons.

"Do you need help back upstairs?"

"Oh, no, I'll make it."

"Do you need anything? Are you sure?"

"I'm just weak and need to lie down."

I quietly regarded her.

"Look Margarite, don't hesitate to call someone if you need anything at all, ok? Let Annie know that you're not feeling well, alright?"

She agreed.

After that we said our goodbyes and she headed back upstairs. I stood watching.

I hated to leave her, but didn't have much of a choice. I was on the clock. I comforted myself with the knowledge that Margarite was a woman of habit and so she had almost certainly talked with several of her friends from church, no doubt asking for prayer. I also felt certain that Annie would come by, so I wasn't too concerned about her being left alone. Nevertheless, I felt uneasy about leaving. But I did.

When I began the route the next day, I looked forward to seeing how Margarite was doing. I had seen her jump back from the flu before in remarkably good time. For an elderly woman, she had an amazing constitution. And since the sun was out and the birds were chirping, she just had to be feeling better. How could anyone be sick with weather like this?

When I arrived at her apartment, I noticed a middle-aged woman standing outside Margarite's door. She wore a plain dress with a long sleeved, white blouse. Her hair was dark and neatly pulled back into a bun. There were also a couple cardboard boxes sitting on the ground near her. When she caught sight of me, she considered my approach with a solemn expression.

"Are you Austin?"

"Yes."

"Hi, I'm Annie. I'm sure you've heard about me." She hesitated and then continued, her words burdened, "I'm sorry to tell you, but Margarite passed away last night."

"What?"

Annie's face looked grim. She dropped her eyes and continued, "When I came here this morning, I found Margarite in her bed. She had apparently passed away during the night."

Margarite was in her mid-nineties, so I shouldn't have been shocked by the news. But it did surprise me. Not even three days ago she was gliding easily up and down her steep steps. Now she was dead.

"What happened?" I asked.

Annie shrugged her shoulders, "She's just old, Austin. It was her time to go."

I rubbed the back of my head, while considering Margarite's apartment.

Annie interrupted my thoughts, "Well, I've already started to clean out some of the food and came across these." She pulled a bag of Fig Newtons from out of one of the boxes on the ground. "I think she would want you to have them."

That was just about more than I could bear. I didn't sob though. In fact, I didn't even cry. But inside I felt the sharp pains of grief gripping my heart. Reluctantly, I reached out and accepted the half empty package of Fig Newtons.

"The funeral will be held in three days at her church."

I nodded, quietly thanked her, and then walked away.

The realization that Margarite was gone didn't fully sink in until the next day. I can remember pausing briefly on the sidewalk, considering her door silently. When you do the same thing for five years, it's hard to suddenly change your routine. So even though I knew she was gone, a strong impulse still urged me to go and ring her doorbell. It was as if my mind couldn't catch up with reality. And so when I continued to walk by her apartment day after day, everything within me ached. It felt wrong to keep going. But there was nothing else to do.

Left to the solitude of my own thoughts, I kept thinking about death. I found myself despising it, not merely death's terrible results- the absence of life, the sting of loss and the utter removal of a person from our realm- but I actually felt an acute hatred for the very thing itself. It was then when I understood more fully the significance of a short passage in the Bible which reads, "The last enemy to be destroyed is death."

Death is an enemy, maybe the worst of enemies. We think of it as something that just is, something natural, something unalterably part of normal life. But it isn't. Or it shouldn't be. It only seems natural because we're merely used to dealing with it. In reality it's horribly unnatural, dreadful beyond measure. It's not how things should be.

Man hates transience, and everything within him recoils at the thought of impermanence. We long for something more. We intuitively know that meaningfulness resides ultimately in the bosom of eternal life. It's in this respect that I honestly don't know how people cope with death apart from God; how they can continue to plod along life's course with the dread of impending death and eternal nothingness ever looming before them. Just think of that: irremediable nothingness; nonexistence forever and ever. Everything we have done, every last detail, swallowed up in the eternal void of the forgotten past.

Consider the words of the famous atheist, Bertrand Russell. In one of his more candid moments he reflected upon the meaninglessness of life in an ultimately materialistic universe. He said, "Brief and powerless is Man's life; on him and all his race the slow, sure doom falls pitiless and dark. Blind to good and evil, reckless of destruction, omnipotent matter rolls on its relentless way; for Man, condemned today to lose his dearest, tomorrow himself to pass through the gate of darkness..."

I shudder to think.

While continuing to walk the sidewalks of City 15, I reflected more deeply upon the wonder and glory of Christ's resurrection, and how it wasn't merely an amazing display of power when He rose on the third day, but the installation of real hope, the first fruits of a guaranteed harvest, an assurance of better things for sinful men, if they will but repent and believe. But it's even yet still more. It's the actual reversal of death itself; life triumphing over decay, grace in action. It is hope. It is true hope. And it provides the human heart, which knows there is more, genuine comfort.

There is more than eternal silence.

The mailman becomes a part of the scenery on his route. As such, he watches children grow up, people trim their bushes, maintain their homes, barbeque, buy new cars, and unfortunately, he watches some of his patrons die as well. That's tough. It's difficult watching Andy Barger's step dad wither away from cancer. One moment he's sitting outside on the porch with Andy's mom waiting for the mail, the next I'm watching him stagger down the street with a cane, terribly thin and gaunt. And then there's my young friend Scotty, a mentally handicapped boy who loved to follow me around on his bike. One night while riding back from the county fair, he was tragically struck by a car. After a few grueling weeks of lying in a coma, he finally succumbed to death. While in this coma, I watched his family grieve the tragedy. I watched them lament their loss. I saw these things because I was their mailman. And because I was their mailman, I felt a measure of their pain.

So while it's true that January brings with it many difficult days, and the humid months of July and August certainly inflict a misery of their own, the truly lasting impressions of grief come from watching close patrons pass away.

Chapter 25

A Twist of Fate

-And I thought the odds of Goldtooth winning the lottery were
astronomical-

Just about every square inch of Little Beirut is familiar to
me. If anything new pops up, I usually notice it. And so when I
rounded the corner of North Pearcy Street and caught sight of an
unfamiliar dog, a small, grayish brown terrier with short hair, I
perked up. He was sitting next to another furry companion, a dog
that I happened to know well; a lazy, mild mannered, off-white
spaniel that spends most of its time stretched out on a porch. I
don't know that he's ever barked at me. That would take too much
energy. But unlike Mr. Lazy, when the new dog spied me out, he
instantly rose to his feet and eyed me. It wasn't a welcoming look.

When confronted with potentially aggressive dogs, I usually
adopt one of three different strategies for handling the situation.
Sometimes I try to coax my canine enemies out of their foul mood
by kissing the air and calling, "Here, boy. Come here, boy," as if we
were longtime friends (of course this is merely a hoax that they often
see straight through). If it's a large, Herculean beast, I'll stop,
casually turn around and walk briskly away. The mail is neatly
bundled up and curtailed until a later date.

On this particular occasion, I chose to ignore the agitated
dog, hoping to convey with each easy stride, "Don't mind me, I'm
just passing through; in fact, I don't even see you, so just chill out,
ok?" This often sets a dog at ease, or at least checks a brewing
tirade. They may growl and bark, but usually keep their distance.

Not so with this dog. As I continued down the sidewalk,
heading straight towards him, he began to tremble with rage. His
legs stiffened and lips contorted. This gave me considerable reason
for concern, but I still felt relatively confident that he wouldn't
charge.

207

I was wrong.

With a tremendous leap he was off and running, teeth flashing, eyes full of hatred, charging like an angry hornet. Something had really set this dog off. I definitely couldn't ignore him any longer.

Since he was small, I decided that mace wouldn't be necessary, at least not right away, and so I kept him at bay with a few short kicks.

"Get out of here! Go on! Git! Git!"

The little booger was persistent and wouldn't back off. It's as if there was a particularly intense hatred propelling the dog, an especially cruel desire for bloodshed urging him on.

In he shot, darting and snapping, floating back and forth like a seasoned boxer.

"Darn it, dog, you had better back off or you're-"

I caught my voice when a skinny man with large glasses came running out, arms waving, shouting "Wait a minute, I'll get him! I'll get him!"

The man scooped up the dog and cradled it close to his chest.

"Oh, I'm so sorry. I didn't think he would do that."

As the man continued to apologize for his pet's behavior, I considered the dog with a squint. Something seemed strangely familiar. I looked hard, staring directly into the dog's dark eyes.

Wait a minute. I've seen those eyes.

I moved in for a closer look, and to my utter amazement, I recognized the face. It was Mac!

The man continued to gush apologies, but I didn't hear a word he was saying. I held up my hand to stop him and asked, "Where did you get that dog?"

The man looked down at the terrier, smiled and said, "Well, about a week ago I went to the pound, and this cute guy caught my attention. The woman told me that he would come with a crate, a bowl and a leash, if I would take him home. That was good enough for me. So here he is. He's my new dog."

Well, there you have it. I'm the first mailman in all of history to have been attacked by a dog that was once his own. I feel so honored. At least my wife would be pleased. Mac had found a new home and seemed to have a bright future promising many days of doggie delights, stretching out on a porch with his new friend, Mr. Sleepy Spaniel, gnawing on my knee caps and whatnot. Our destinies appeared to be inextricably intertwined, bound together by a grinning providence.

To think that I didn't mace him when I had the chance.

As the man rubbed Mac's neck, chuckling at the irony, I stood speechless.

Mac's new owner looked down at the little terrier and asked, "What did you name him?"

"Huh?"

"What did you name him?"

"Mac," I replied.

He nodded in agreement.

"I like that. I think I'll call him Big Mac. Yeah, Big Mac. That sounds good."

Epilogue

"Neither snow nor rain nor heat nor gloom of night stays these couriers from the swift completion of their appointed rounds."

-Inscription found on the General Post Office in New York City at 8th Avenue and 33rd Street-

———————

If you've made it this far into the book, then I want to congratulate you, for you have faithfully journeyed through each chapter. You've read them all. And so now you know what it's really like to walk with the mailman[4].

I'm hoping that by now it's clear that the sidewalks of America are a place of high adventure and intrigue, a place where the average citizen roams wild, unhindered and real. I want you to think Neil Armstrong, Shackleton, Lewis and Clark... the Mailman. I'm hoping that you think of each individual lawn as a pathway into someone else's little world, a trek into the bizarre and the unique, a journey into true American culture. You may not want to go there, and honestly, I don't blame you. Really the only reason I do it is for the money. But never mind that. It's still a great job, and I can hardly imagine doing anything else. Of course it wouldn't break my heart if millions decided to buy this book. Actually, it would be pretty exciting if someone other than my mom, and maybe the four or five people she'll coerce into reading this, as well as a few of my other close relatives, decided to purchase it. At any rate, I don't think Harry Potter has anything to worry about.

Realistically, it looks like I'm going to retire as a mailman. That's not a horrible thought. But who knows if I'll be able to make it. Since I hired in at such a young age (you might recall that I was

———————

[4] If you want to take an advanced course in mail delivery, all that is required is for you to allow yourself to be chewed on by a dozen or so stray dogs, bury yourself in a snow bank until hypothermia sets in, suffer a few thousand paper cuts and repeatedly bang your head against a brick wall, as this last requirement will simulate dealings with management.

nineteen years old), I still have a very, very long way to go. A gal I work with has one of those retirement clocks sitting on her case. It's a constant reminder of how much time, right down to the actual second, is left before the bliss of never having to carry another relay becomes a reality. Curious, I went online and used a similar program to calculate the number of remaining days. When I punched in my retirement date, it read: 10^{40}.

I try not to think about it anymore.

So anyway, I'm not sure I can make it. Not merely because it's so far away, but because I'm not sure my body will be able to hold up. When I look around at some of the carriers who have been walking for twenty or more years, they're hunched over like Quasimodo and can be seen hobbling around, popping pain killers by the handfuls. Others have a permanent tilt to their shoulders from carrying a bag on one side for too long. It's not a pretty sight. And so I'm wondering if by the time retirement actually rolls around, I might have a bionic leg or arm. That's kind of a cool thought though. Just think how surprised a dog would be if he were to chomp onto a titanium leg? But who knows, since my father is a chiropractor, I just might have a chance of making it in one straight piece.

I am a little concerned about my toes, however. After fourteen years of walking, apparently from all the friction, I have acquired some serious calluses. I'm guessing that this is normal for carriers, but on the top of each of my big toes, right at the joint, are two thick, leathery, none-too-attractive, prominent pads. Although my wife finds them disgusting, she nevertheless harbors a certain morbid curiosity towards them, sometimes poking them with a stick, wondering if they might be alive or if they could be filed down. Maybe by retirement they'll be large enough to earn me a spot on one of those doctor shows where they take patients with large goiters or enormous tumors and fix them up.

All in all, the future looks pretty bright. Sooner or later I'll land one of those all driving routes and be able to cruise around without a care in the world. Maybe I'll fatten up too, and winter won't seem so bad. And as a mailman, I'll always know the latest gossip- which celebrity is in rehab, or getting married, or cheating, or getting fat. The mailman can't help but know these things, because when he has to look at the same magazine covers over and over again, first while casing them up, and then while delivering them, he inevitably absorbs the information, willing or not. Just ask a mailman what Brad Pitt is up to. He'll know. Ask him who has been named the most gorgeous individual in America. He'll know. Newspaper headlines, crazy tabloids, Newsweek, Time, People, RedBook, he sees them all. Well, nearly all of them. I can't say that I ever delivered a single Pottery Barn catalog or Wall Street Journal to the inhabitants of Little Beirut. Playboys were more the magazine of choice.

Now if you'll permit me to end on a more serious note, I really do want to say just how thankful I am for the United States Postal Service. Overall, it's a great job, and I consider myself truly blessed. I'm also proud of my profession, and I can better understand why my family was so excited when I landed the job. And while we mailmen don't have quite as cool a motto as the Navy Seals with their, "Leave no man behind," we do have, "The mail must go through." There's a ring of honor in that.

So seeing how I'm presently scratching out these final thoughts on a scrap piece of paper while standing at the back of my postal truck, sweat rolling down my face from the late summer heat, bag loaded and heavy on my shoulder, I had better quite wasting time and perform my duties. The mail must go through.

Appendix

The Blueness of the Uniform

"It was the whiteness of the whale that above all things appalled me."

-Moby Dick, chapter 42-

There is a sublime and peculiar quality regarding the mailman that has hitherto been overlooked, a certain attribute that, if I were to disregard and cap my pen, would leave the reader in an unfortunate state of want, for he would be deprived of certain postal glories. And so desiring not to orphan my readers by neglecting such a sweet topic, I must endeavor toward an explanation, to shed some light on the genius of the mailman's uniform; though not the uniform in its strict design, per se, although there is an excellence to be found there, but rather in the choice of the color blue. Yes. It is the color blue of which we shall speak, that shade which sets the mailman apart from all others and which endows him with greatness. But how can I hope to explain myself here; and yet in some dim, random way, explain myself I must, else all these chapters might be for naught.

In nature one will observe that the color blue has been endowed with a certain preeminence, as though it were meant to be esteemed, or praised, or exalted to a place of special honor, destined to enjoy a lofty position whereby it looks down on those other colors, even inspiring colors like red and green and sun-fire orange, and declare, "Stretch out and fill the earth, all ye magnificent shades; paint the landscape, paint and brush; but as you do, remember this: The sky is my playground."

Stand out in a grassy field and look up at that playground, dear reader. What fills the canvas? Blue, I tell you. Boundless, endless blue. It is blue that peeks through the mighty Redwoods, dons the mountaintops, directs the clouds and cradles the sun. It is a blue so pervasive that one observing our planet from some inestimable distance will point and declare, "Look there! A pale blue dot."

So is it mere coincidence that the Almighty, when He created the expanse and marked off its boundaries on the second day, chose blue from His palette? No. It is no mere coincidence. By divine decree, that would be the color chosen to mark off the firmament and instill within men a sense of wonder. The sky would be, as the Psalmist says, that which proclaims His handiwork; for day after day it pours forth its speech, and night after night it reveals its knowledge, and its voice goes out unto all the earth.

But lest we think the ground beneath our feet offsets the predominance of blue above, thereby balancing the world, merely escape from the anchor of land and venture out into the vast watery places. Stand atop the mast. Look into the mouth of the ocean. Peer towards the horizon. Twirl the compass. There one will find himself standing in a complete and perfect globe of blue. Is it no wonder that men seek such visions, leaning against pier heads and railings, fixing their gazes like silent sentinels, abandoning themselves in ocean reveries? Is it not because of all the blue?

But this is only the beginning. Within the ranks of the animal kingdom, blue likewise entertains a lordly office. Consider the peacock in his proud estate. Splaying his royal colors in rainbow arc, he dazzles the eye with whimsy and splash. But note what stands like a sculpture at the center of the stage? Is it not the brilliant figure of the peacock dressed in solid blue? Does he not rear his proud head because of this color?

Or what of the Snub-Nosed Monkey of eastern Tibet, that agile creature of the tree tops whose face burns like an inner flame; or the fierce Mandrill of Southern Cameroon, that warrior of the jungle whose nose resembles that of an Indian made ready for war? Yes, it is the careful positioning of blue that magnifies the creature's excellence and impresses upon us a sense of authority and regality.

We may likewise ask what startles the young child when he peers into the robin's nest? Is it not the blueness of the eggs? Are they not little Neptunes in a basket? Or what is more shocking than the darting tongue of the Australian Skink? Is there a brighter cord in the seamstress' cabinet?

Shall I mention the Agama of Thailand, the Rainbow Lory, the Blue-bellied Roller, the long-curved beak of the Honeycreeper, the flamboyant wings of the Spicebush Swallowtail, the titanic Blue Whale, or the austere glance of the Victoria Crowned Pigeon? Are we not constrained to admit that it is the color blue that endows such creatures with special glory?

So yes, we may look to the skies above, even to the northern auroras that dance in the cold night, or to the creatures that crawl across the face of the earth, or to the hyacinths that dot the hillside, those flowers which speak of rebirth, yes, we may consider all such places, but we must also look within the earth itself where men burrow and tunnel for those rare stones of precious value. Here one may certainly think of the ruby with its fiery eyes, or the emerald with its turquoise crown, but we dare not, indeed, cannot overlook the sapphire, that tutor of impenetrable blue. Look into its depths. What do you see? Nothing but infinite azure; nothing but oceanic blue wrapped in arctic blush. It is Himalayan, the deepest and most Medusa of blues, transfixing in its gaze and shimmering with the meridian flare of a thousand blossoms. Bottomless is that chamber of refracting blues; a coiling labyrinth where the eye wanders like a wraith in an ethereal blue of forgotten mists.

We could venture further, exploring the wonder of the young, blue-eyed Norwegians of Stavanger, the curtains of the tabernacle, Aaron's ephod, Mongolian dye, Roman prefects, Egyptian sails, Mordecai's royal garments, and an endless assemblage of other glorious things, but we need not. By now it should be clear that when confronted with the task of choosing a color out of the vast array of hues and counter hues, the postal divines, by an ineffable and sublime process, chose their course wisely, securing for the mailman that color most highly esteemed, the color blue.

But here it is a frightful thing to contemplate just how far they could have fallen. For suppose they had chosen a different color. Suppose for a moment, perhaps due to their drinking some foul substance, or smoking some arcane matter, or their coming under the influence of a diabolical spirit, that it entered their minds to choose the color brown. Can you imagine it? Can you imagine a uniform consisting entirely of brown? I shudder to think. And by extension, can you imagine trading in the patriotic colors of the postal truck for a flat and abysmal, dark brown?

It is scarcely conceivable.

Now it should be plain to all those possessing a sober mind that just as the color blue invokes glory, so too, but in a fatefully ignominious way, the color brown effectually impresses upon us dire connections.

Here one need only recall the days of righteous Noah when the doors of the ark were sealed shut and the heavens and fountains of the deep burst forth. As the eternal springs filled the earth, and as the terrible deluge buried men in their watery graves, the churning waters with its disturbed sediments and earthy bits no doubt painted the oceans a murky brown; an awful, muddy, judgment filled brown[5].

I ask, is there not more terror to be found in waters dyed brown? Merely consider those American explores of old who stumbled upon the Colorado River. Looking down from the ravine's edge, were they not struck by the brown quality of those furious rapids; those foaming, violent, gesticulating torrents of earthen hue? And even in the case of calmer waters, isn't the dread of approaching an African water hole heightened by the muddy veil? Scarcely can a man judge the lurkings beneath such a surface. Nor can we shake the frightful image of the hand grasping and clutching for life as the slow swallow of quicksand digests its prey.

Surely judgment and dread are wed in an awful matrimony of brown pigmentation. But this is not all. Lift the stem of a rotting plant, raise the bruised apple before the eye, consider the foul decomposition of the fallen animal; is there not a fixed correlation between this hue and decay?

There grows the flower on the lilied bank, opening its bright plumage for all the world to see. But wait! A withering effect sets in. The flower falters; it begins to die. What is this common effect that befalls such serene blossoms? Is it not the sarcophagus touch

---

[5] Here it should be noted that as the sediments slowly settled, and as the angry tempests subsided, a fresh restoration of blue thereby followed, rejuvenating both sea and air to their original estates. And when Noah emerged from the battered vessel, he beheld that covenantal sign etched into the horizon, the majestic rainbow, that brilliant arc of promise where the color blue runs its course like a king in a fiery chariot.

attended with brown? But go further. Watch the camel rider of central Mali cross that arid vastness known as the great Sahara. Circumambulating the dusty mounds with wrapped face and squinting eyes, what does he behold but a measureless congregation of brown sand. Truly it is an oceanic wasteland where the minds of men are driven to insanity. Here many suppose such madness is due to the exhausting heat; and this true, but only in part. The poor wandering soul in that ubiquity of brown suffers what the Eskimos have learned in the arctic. But unlike snow blindness, the persistent sight of brown drives the traveler to irredeemable madness. Yes, it is the constant sight of the swirling sand that tips sanity.

Long have men naturally recognized another grim association, adorning themselves with sackcloth in order to image that dust to dust and ashes to ashes which all men are destined to taste. There goes the funeral procession with the casket of the deceased. There go the wailing women and the men beating their chests. It is a dismal sight of death and tear soaked brown. And where is that brown coffin placed? It is placed in the bowls of the earth where the earthworms roam and the roots snake; a hidden world of clay and dirt; a world thankfully concealed by green grass.

But if all this were not enough, there remains one final proof so convincing, so utterly unassailable, that the mere mention of it stops all complaints. And while it is true that there exists some variation in this species- some being white or black or spotted- the dominance of brown demands no argument, as even the youngest of children know this truth. So consider lastly, and above all else, that it is the dog himself who is most commonly colored brown.

That, dear reader, is more potent than a thousand Saharas.

Even in the face of all that has been said, I suppose one might vainly imagine, or strangely expect, there to be a certain similitude between the package itself and the one delivering it, which is to say that maybe the delivery man's uniform should be brown like the parcel he carries. But of course, this is sheer folly. Shall the mortician resemble the dead? Or shall the veterinarian grow fur? Would the cook comb his hair into a cabbage? Indeed, the parcel is but a temporary shell meant to be torn and tossed into the fire. So why garnish one's personage in the likeness of such a thing? Dost thou desire to be tossed into the garbage bin?

So given all that has been set down in an orderly and careful manner, and given the abundant wisdom of the postal ancients, and the awful connections between the color brown and judgment, death, decay, and the dog, it must be asked, and it must be asked truly, what can brown do for you?

I love a good laugh. This book is proof of that. But life is often a strange mixture of humor and heartbreak, sorrow and joy. There are good times, and there are times of great challenge. There are times to joke around, and there are times for sober reflection.

Here I'm asking for a moment of sober reflection.

It goes without saying that some of the most challenging events in life come in the form of sickness. This is especially the case when a loved one is involved. Few things are more difficult than to sit beside the bed of a spouse or a child and watch them battle a disease. It is hard, in part, because our hands are often tied. We wish we could switch spots with them, or somehow give them a portion of our life, or health, or strength. If we could just do more somehow...

Sometimes, however, we can't do more. That is true.

But sometimes we can.

I'd like to introduce you to the *Be The Match Foundation*®, an organization dedicated to helping people do that something more. Through this organization, men and women are provided a unique opportunity to help in a way that goes beyond writing a check or sending a get well card. The foundation provides an opportunity to perform a truly profound act, an act that can literally save a life.

How so? You do this by giving part of yourself for another. You do this by donating bone marrow or cord blood to those who most need it. You give sacrificially.

I want to encourage you to seriously consider helping someone who is battling a life-threatening disease. To give them hope. To be a hero. A real hero.

So let me challenge you. Consider joining this foundation by being willing to give the gift of life to another in real need. By purchasing this book, you have already helped in a small way, as a portion of the proceeds will help benefit the foundation. But I want to urge you to go deeper. Be a match. Check out their website. Talk with them. Sign up. And make a real and lasting difference.

You can visit them here:

www.BeTheMatchFoundation.org